12.95

D1120602

MILITARY TO CIVILIAN TRANSITION
JOB
Search Strategies

Dorch, Patricia

Military to Civilian Transition: Job Search Strategies and Tips to Get Hired in the Civilian Job Market/Patricia Dorch

Bulk Purchases: Minimum Order – 50 Books
For information about discounts for bulk purchases please contact Patricia Dorch at:

Website: www.militarytociviliantransition.net
Email: Patricia@militarytociviliantransition.net

Website: www.Whatisprofessionalism.com
Email: Patricia@Whatisprofessionalism.com

Website: www.execudress.com
Email: Patricia@execudress.com

Printed in the United States of America

ISBN – 13: 978-0-9816854-7-2
ISBN – 10: 0-9816854-7-1

DEDICATION

This book is dedicated to Willie Mae Dorch,
Francine Dorch,
and
In Memory of Norman Dorch

MILITARY DEDICATION

This book is dedicated to all Military Men and Women - Veterans, Wounded Veterans, and Disabled Veterans who have served in the Armed Forces. Thank you for your service, sacrifice, dedication and bravery – you are our heroes.

ACKNOWLEDGEMENT

I want to extend my personal and sincere thanks to all who have dedicated their time, expertise and advice for this book. Your knowledge and support have contributed to my success.

CONTENTS

"A Mission to Get Hired."
- PATRICIA DORCH

"Knowledge and Transferable Skills
Are Your Most Valuable Assets to Get Hired."
-PATRICIA DORCH

"A Mission to Get Hired"

-PATRICIA DORCH

Military to Civilian Transition Job Search Strategies and Tips to Get Hired in the Civilian Job Market

INTRODUCTION

Are you looking for a roadmap to market your transferable skills in the civilian job market? The information in *Military to Civilian Transition: Job Search Strategies and Tips to Get Hired in the Civilian Job Market* is a career resource that eliminates the time and learning curve involved with identifying successful strategies to maximize your job search.

Do you need new interview strategies to "market" your Military experience to a civilian employer?

In the Military you presented ideas and strategies to officers, peers and civilians to accomplish daily goals. The skills you used in the Military are transferable to the civilian job market. Use transferable skills to illustrate to civilian employers you are the most qualified candidate for the job.

Use examples of transferable skills in a "short story" format with a civilian employer. Can you tell a good story?

Every Military person has a good story to tell. Communicate in a "short story" format how you used *specific transferable* skills in the Military by providing "examples" of your achievements. Describe how you – solved a problem, re-routed a shipment, prepared a new report, used good judgment in re-assigning a project to another solider, changed a procedure to create a more efficient outcome, planned and executed a special assignment and transported equipment or troops to achieve field goals.

Based on the job description use examples how your Military experience is transferable to the civilian job market. Short stories distinguish you from other candidates and essential to communicating how your *knowledge, skills* and *abilities* were used to achieve daily goals. For each skill required in the job description – during your interview provide a short story how you used the transferable skill.

What does your body language communicate to employers about you?

Are you aware of your non-verbal communication? Are you confident or anxious? Do you communicate interest, lack of interest, arrogance or entitlement about the career opportunity?

Employers place emphasis on whether or not you are the "right fit" for their organization.

The candidate who has exceptional skills is only part of the employer's goal. Assessing your personality and body language during the interview is important in identifying whether you are the right fit for the company culture.

The Power of Personal Branding - Do you have a personal brand?

How do you "stand out" from your interview competition and your peers? To attract the ideal civilian employer use secret strategies to build your personal brand and position you for career success. During your interview communicate what makes your personal brand distinct, unique, exceptional, compelling, engaging and valuable to an organization. Learn fifteen strategies to build your brand personality to "stand out" in today's competitive job market.

Do you know how to close the interview and Ask For The Job™?

Closing the interview is the most important step in getting what you want – the job offer. It's not enough for a job seeker in any market to ask what the next step is in the interview process; focus on the purpose for which you are interviewing and that is to land the job offer.

You can not get what you want unless you Ask For The Job™. Asking the employer for the job opens the door for a job offer. Do not assume the interviewer knows you want the job; express what you want by being professional and direct. If you want the job – ask for it. It's not what you say; it's how you say it in your communication, presentation, tone, eye contact, body language and sincerity. Learn the *secret* words to Ask For The Job™ and get hired!

Military to Civilian Transition is written to help you revamp your current job search strategy to be successful, get hired and promoted throughout your career.

Everything you need to accomplish your mission is in *Military to Civilian Transition: Job Search Strategies and Tips to Get Hired in the Civilian Job Market.*

"Show you mean business."

-PATRICIA DORCH

STRATEGY ONE

Power Interview Image Investment Strategy

INTRODUCTION

Do you have an interview suit? Planning your interview wardrobe is essential in conveying to the hiring manager you are serious about your career. Every candidate should have a quality "interview suit" and shoes reserved in his or her wardrobe for interviews. A navy blue, tailored suit makes a powerful first impression followed by a black or charcoal gray for future interviews. Add a blouse for women and a shirt and tie for men to "show you mean business" in the eyes of the hiring committee.

Although women's pant suits are widely accepted in the workplace, a "skirt suit" depending on the industry may be more favorable during the interview process. Use good judgment in determining whether or not you should wear a pant suit for your first interview. Once you have achieved your new career, a pant suit (if appropriate for the work environment) adds an alternative business or business casual look.

During multiple interviews, be consistent in your appearance; wear suits, *not* separates or coordinates. Your attention to detail in the final interview phase is crucial to your success. Close the interview with your ability to perform the job. Once hired project the same professional image you presented during your interview. Your image is an investment strategy for success.

Civilian Men

Suit

- Solid color or small stripes
- Matching jacket and trousers
- Trousers cuffed

Shirt

- Modified spread collar
- White
- Long-sleeved

Tie

- Solid, stripes or small patterns
- Conservative
- No red (red is the color of power)

Shoes

- Lace-ups only
- Dark color

- Polished and in good condition

Socks

- Dark color
- Match to trousers or shoes
- Mid-calf

Belt

- Match to trousers or shoes
- No braces (suspenders)

Jewelry

- Earrings – not recommended
- Bracelets – not recommended

Hair

- Cut and styled
- Facial hair trimmed and groomed (you may consider removing beards and side burns during the interview process)

Fragrance

- No cologne or scented aftershave

Nail Care

- Manicured

- Neatly trimmed
- Clear polish (optional)

Attache Case (Optional)

- Leather
- Dark color – black or dark brown
- Stylish
- Not oversized

Civilian Women

Suit

- Conservative
- Solid color or small stripes
- Skirt suit – recommended
- Pant suit – optional
- No red or fashion colors

Blouse

- Solid or small print or stripe
- No turtlenecks

Shoes

- Classic leather pumps – a low heel is recommended over flat styles
- Closed-toe – recommended

- Dark color
- Polished and in good condition

Jewelry

- No ankle bracelets

Hair

- Professionally styled
- No fashion hair colors

Hose

- Coordinated with attire
- No bare legs

Makeup

- Conservative application

Fragrance

- None

Nail Care

- Manicure or acrylic fills – no chipped nail polish
- No black, fashion bright colors or studs
- No long nails

Attache Case (Optional)

- Leather or soft style
- Dark color – preferably black or dark brown
- Stylish
- Not oversized

Civilian Business Tools for Success – Men and Women

- Leather writing tablet – dark color
- Quality ink pen
- Your personal name badge
- Your personal business card
- Cell phone – TURN OFF (recommended you leave in your vehicle)

How Do I Look?

Image Secrets for Success

INTRODUCTION

Image is everything – it communicates whether you are successful or not. Changes in your wardrobe, accessories and personal grooming are essential to getting hired, promoted and accomplishing your career goals. Use image makeover secrets to improve your visual presentation.

Professional stylish changes will make a big difference in the way you look, feel and how others perceive you. Discuss your image with someone you trust and admire how they dress. Consult with experts such as a sales associate, hair stylist, barber or personal shopper who will assist you in creating a new look.

A personal shopper at fine department stores provides wardrobe recommendations for your body type, industry and age group – usually complimentary. Stores that do not have personal shoppers – ask a sales associate for assistance at warehouse stores, outlet stores and men's or women's departments.

How Do I Look?

Your image and everything you say and do should create the perception that you are professional, intelligent, reliable, skilled, trustworthy and polished. Take time to do an assessment of how you look. When you prepare your wardrobe for an interview, promotion or regular business day ask yourself:

1. What image do I project?

2. Will my image get me hired?

3. Will my image increase my salary offer?

4. Does my image make me feel and look respected?

5. Does my image help position me for promotions?

6. Does my image attract the wrong type of attention?

7. Does my image help identify me to take a possible leadership role in the absence of management?

8. With whom am I meeting today? Will I be meeting a customer, vendor or visitor at my location or theirs? If either applies, it is recommended you dress "business", although it may be your company business casual day. When meeting with a client at their location on their designated business casual or casual day – dress in business attire. You never know what other guests may be attending your meeting without your knowledge. First impressions do count.

9. Does my image prepare me for unannounced meetings, internal or external visitors?

10. Does my image promote career success or failure?

Civilian Men

INTRODUCTION

Is your image costing you a career opportunity? There is power in first impressions – people treat you differently based on what they see. You will feel more confident during an interview and be more successful at work when you improve your image. A professional image and polished grooming can increase your salary and chances of accomplishing your career goals. Listed are secrets to manage your image.

Secret 1: Business Suits and Coordinates

- Suit – jacket and slacks in the same color and fabric
- Coordinates – jacket or slacks in different fabrics and colors
- Waist – not too tight around your waist or mid-section – increase the size if necessary
- Slacks – creased and cuffed
- Slacks –not too tight around your thighs – consider a different style
- Pleated slacks – do not wear pleated waist slacks if you have a full waistline – it draws attention to your waist and makes you look larger
- Baggy looks – not recommended for business
- Button jackets – wear one, two or more button jacket styles based on your body type and preference

- Double breasted jacket style – not recommended for all body types. Consult with a personal shopper or sales associate.
- Jackets – Short jacket styles look best on certain body types. Consult with a personal shopper or sales associate about the style that looks best on you.

Secret 2: Dress Shirt

- Long-sleeved button cuff – recommended for business
- Long-sleeved French cuff – executive look optional
- Modified spread collar – collars that are not buttoned down – recommended for business
- Buttoned down collar – alternative business option
- Dry clean shirts or press shirts that you wash at home – permanent press is not 100% wrinkle free

Secret 3: Undershirt

- Undershirts protect against perspiration and gives body to your dress shirt
- Short sleeve crew neck style undershirts – recommended for business
- Sleeveless undershirts show through your dress shirt – it shows the outline of the neckline and armholes on your chest and back – optional

Secret 4: Neckwear

- Silk fabric is recommended
- Avoid designs that include politics, religion or sexual statements

Secret 5: Shoes

- Stylish
- Lace-up styles for business
- Slip-on styles for business casual (optional)
- Polished in good condition – no worn heels, soles or scuff marks

Secret 6: Socks

- Mid-calf – to avoid showing your leg skin when you sit down
- White socks – wear only for medical reasons – cover with colored socks for a business look

Secret 7: Belt and Braces (suspenders)

- Belt – match to slacks or shoes
- Braces – wear only if you are in good physical shape. If you have a full waistline it will draw attention to that area of your body.

Secret 8: Jewelry and Fragrance

- Earrings – not recommended for business (optional)
- Lip, tongue, nose or chin earrings – not recommended unless for religious reasons

- Body piercing – not recommended for business unless for religious reasons
- Bracelets – not recommended for business
- Watch – in good condition - optional
- Necklace – invisible to others – do not wear on the outside of your shirt
- Cufflinks – engrave your initials for personal branding
- Fragrance – cologne or aftershave – conservative application – be considerate of those who may have allergies – optional

Secret 9: Hair

- New barber or hairstylist – use these options to help you improve your image
- Cut and style – experience new looks
- Clean look – a natural alternative
- Gray hair – consider a color or style change
- Hair style magazines – discuss new ideas with your hair stylist, friends or family

Secret 10: Personal Grooming

Consult with your barber or hair stylist for a polished groomed look.

- Mustache – trimmed and well groomed
- Beard – trimmed and well groomed
- Side burns – trimmed and well groomed
- Goatee – trimmed and well groomed
- Eyebrows – consult with a professional to trim

and shape thick and bushy eyebrows for a groomed look

- Visible nose hairs – carefully trim or consult with a professional to remove

Secret 11: Nails and Hand Care

- Manicure – recommended every two weeks for a professional look
- Oil manicure – keeps cuticles from becoming dry and cracked – costs a little more
- Neatly trimmed – no long nails
- Clear polish – optional
- Schedule an appointment for the best service – takes 30-45 minutes
- Hands – use a light application of a moisturizer to prevent drying and increase smoothness

Secret 12: Lips

- Use lip balm to prevent dry lips – optional
- Be aware of white saliva pockets that may form in the corners of your mouth

Civilian Women

INTRODUCTION

What does your image say about you? You say more than you think – based on how you look. Use your image to build confidence and get what you want – a new job, promotion or recognized for your achievements. Listed are secrets to manage your image.

Secret 1: Business Suit and Coordinates

- Skirt Suit
- Pant Suit
- Fashionable classics
- Colors that compliment you
- Coordinates – wear coordinates to maximize your wardrobe
- Styles – wear fashionable styles appropriate for your age, body type and industry

Secret 2: Blouse, Tops and Sweater Sets

- Blouses – solids, prints and stripes
- Turtlenecks
- Sweater sets
- Sleeveless looks – Optional – Cover sleeveless looks with sweaters, jackets or other tops. Sleeveless looks are recommended only if your arms are in good shape – you will attract the wrong attention if they are not.

Secret 3: Business Dress

- Solids, prints and stripes
- Wear dresses with a jacket or sweater look for business – optional

Secret 4: Business Shoes

- Polished in good condition – no worn heels, soles or scuff marks
- Fashionable business styles
- Closed-toe
- Open-toe – optional based on personal preference and industry
- High, medium, or low heels – personal preference
- Flat heels – optional – do not wear on a daily basis if you are in management role unless for medical reasons.
- You appear more powerful with a low heel rather than with flat styles.

Secret 5: Jewelry, Accessories and Fragrance

- Fashionable jewelry and accessories
- No ankle bracelets
- Rings – limit two rings per hand
- Necklace – limit one necklace
- Earrings – limit two on each ear
- Lip, tongue, nose or chin earrings – not recommended unless for religious reasons

- Body piercing – not recommended for business unless for religious reasons
- Fragrance – conservative application – be considerate of those who may have allergies – optional

Secret 6: Hair

- Expert – consult with your hair stylist for a new look
- Trimmed and styled
- Hair colors – no fashion hair colors or extensions such as – bright red, orange and other trendy or edgy colors
- Extensions, Weaves and Wigs – maintained, clean and styled
- Natural, braids and dreadlocks looks – maintained, clean and styled

Secret 7: Hose

- Coordinated with attire
- Bare legs – optional - personal and business decision

Secret 8: Lips

- Lipstick or lip balm – optional
- Natural look – no lipstick or lip balm – optional

Secret 9: Makeup

- Conservative application
- Natural look - optional

Secret 10: Nails and Hand Care

- Manicure or acrylic fills – no chipped nail polish
- Pedicure – match your toe nail polish to your fingernail polish if you wear open-toe shoes unless you wear a neutral color
- No trendy colors or studs – may distract from your professional image
- No long nails
- Hands – use a light application of a moisturizer to prevent drying and increase softness

Secret 11: Personal Grooming

- Lip hair – consult with a professional for wax removal or another recommended method
- Eyebrows – consult with a professional for trimming and shaping – optional
- Facial Hair – consult with a professional for facial hair removal – optional
- Underarm hair – shave or consult with a professional for underarm hair removal if you wear sleeveless attire uncovered by a jacket or sweater look – personal choice
- Leg Hair – shave or consult with a professional for leg hair removal – personal choice

Secret 12: Casual Attire for Civilian Men and Women

What Not to Wear for Business and Business Casual

Never underestimate the power of your image.

Employees who choose to wear casual attire regardless of the dress policy do so at the risk of limiting their career opportunities. Taking the initiative to improve your image will increase your chances of being promoted and make you more marketable and successful inside and outside of your organization.

There are outlet, discount stores, seasonal sales, weekend, and end of season sales, holiday sales and resale shops available to purchase fashionable affordable attire on a budget.

Before you wear any of the listed attire, consider your career, the amount of money you want to make and ask yourself will this attire advance my career. Listed are styles, accessories and looks that are *not* considered business or business casual.

What Not to Wear for Business or Business Casual

Athletic Wear, Athletic Shoes, Sweatshirts, Sweatpants, Skorts, Shorts, Bermuda Shorts, Tee Shirts, Tank Tops or Nightwear Looks, Spaghetti Straps and/or Sun Dresses, Leggings and/or Spandex Pants, Sheer Clothing, Ankle Bracelets, Fashion Hair Colors, Oversized Baggy and Undersized Clothing, Camouflage Looks, Lounge Style

Wear, Moccasins, Clogs, and any color Flip Flops, Visible Body Art, Tattoos and Piercing.

Secret 13: Self Expression Statements – Civilian Men and Women

Body Art, Tattoos and Piercings

Do you have a tattoo?

Body art, tattoos and piercings are no longer reserved for bikers and sailors. These forms of non-religious "self-expression" statements have made their way to the Military, boardroom and general population of organizations. *However, self-expression statements can cross the business line and form unfavorable perceptions about your professionalism and business judgment.*

Body art, tattoos and piercings that have religious, ethnic and cultural meaning fall into a separate category.

If you have questions about the appropriateness of body art, tattoos and piercings as a "self-expression" or religious, ethnic or cultural statement, contact your company representative for clarification.

During business hours, consider covering non-religious "self-expression" statements of body art and tattoos with attire or makeup and remove body piercing that can be visible on your:

- Face
- Neckline
- Arms

- Wrists
- Hands
- Waistline
- Thighs
- Legs
- Ankles

Bonus Secrets for Civilian Men and Women

Secret 1: Appearances Do Count!

It takes less than ten seconds for someone to form an impression of you based on what they see.

Appearance is based on the following percentages and characteristics:

- **55%** - Appearance and body language
- **38%** - Vocal tone, pacing and voice inflection
- **7%** - Verbal Message

Secret 2: Image Sizing

- Wear attire that fits properly
- Use a tailor for alterations to achieve a custom fit

Secret 3: Quality Brands and Dry Cleaning Service

- Quality brands communicates success while inexpensive brands implies the opposite
- Quality brands tend to be more generous in how the size fits

- Big, tall and plus sizes – invest in quality purchases
- Dry cleaning – invest in a quality dry cleaning service. Avoid inexpensive services – their cleaning method may shrink or discolor your quality attire.

Secret 4: Business Image Tools

- Leather writing tablet (black or dark brown with two business cards holders)
- Quality brand pen and pencil set (name engraving adds a personal touch)
- Business card and holder
- Personal name badge
- Cell phone – *Turn Off* – or put on vibrate during meetings, conferences and use good judgment at work

Summary

How do you look? You may be paid less than your peers, overlooked for a new job or promotion if your image is not appropriate for a new position.

Do you resist change?

Change is uncomfortable whether it's at work, in your personal life and especially your appearance. The first step in making a change in your image is to be open to new ideas that will give you a new look. Changes in your image can have a big impact on your career, future and your secret for success.

Interview Etiquette

18 Rules for Interviewing

INTRODUCTION

Organizations commit a considerable amount of time and resources interviewing and recruiting employees. Their goal is to identify your *knowledge, skills,* and *abilities* to determine whether you are the best candidate for the job.

How to provide examples of your transferable skills to employers

Your goal is to demonstrate how your experience can be of value to their organization. Provide examples of how your *knowledge, skills,* and *abilities* will help position you as a qualified candidate for the job. Use examples of past performance in Military and civilian experiences such as - project management, special assignments, hobbies, volunteer work, community work, leadership, supervisory or management positions and other activities to assist you in communicating your achievements.

At your interview, a professional appearance is the first impression you make; your manners and professionalism become important afterwards. Usually, the combination of *appearance, manners,* and *professionalism* help form the interview's hiring decision. Learn the etiquette rules of interviewing to assist you in becoming more successful in achieving career goals.

18 Rules for Interviewing

Rule 1 – Appearance

- Wear a professional business suit with a matching top and bottom in the same fabric.
- Women have the option of wearing a skirt or pant suit.

Rule 2 – Be On Time

- The interviewer interprets your arrival of fifteen to twenty minutes early, as your interest, commitment, dependability, and professionalism. Being late can show the opposite.

Rule 3 – First Impression

- Be kind to the receptionist.
- Do not smoke, use your cell phone, chew gum, or listen to a portable radio while you are waiting for your interview.
- You are being observed by the receptionist and cameras.

Rule 4 – Outer Coat

- Do not wear your outer coat into the interview.
- Take your coat off after you have spoken to the receptionist.

Rule 5 – Introductions

- If the interviewer uses both first and last name during introductions, use the last name when addressing him or her.
- Introduce yourself by the name you *prefer* to be called.

Rule 6 – Handshake

- Give a confident handshake, direct eye contact and smile when you shake hands.
- If you have sweaty palms dry them with a tissue prior to your introduction.

Rule 7 – Sitting Down

- Do not sit down until you have been invited to do so. *Ask* where they would like you to sit if there are multiple chairs.

Rule 8 – Preparing for the Interview

- What skills does the position require?
- What skills do you have that relate to the job description?
- What anecdotes can you tell about your knowledge, skills, and abilities that demonstrate your qualifications?
- Before the interview, identify two or three top-selling points you want the interviewer to know about you, and determine how to present them during the interview.

- Bring three copies of your resume, even though you know they already have a copy. Multiple resume copies prepare you for unexpected group interviews.
- Bring a leather writing portfolio and a quality pen with black ink.
- Review your resume prior to the interview. Be prepared to answer questions and explain any gaps during your employment.
- Prepare and memorize five to seven quality questions you can ask about the position.
- Research the company and department of interest and know who the key people are.
- Identify who has the power to hire you.

Rule 9 – Vocal Tone

- Match your vocal tone to the interviewer. Do not talk too loud or whisper when you speak.

Rule 10 – Body Language

Avoid signs of negative or power body language:

- Slouching
- Avoiding Eye Contact
- Forced Smiles
- Swinging of Foot or Legs
- Crossing your Legs over your Thigh – may be interpreted as a power statement
- Hand or Finger Movements

Rule 11 – Eye Contact

- Make eye contact, show self-confidence, and answer questions directly with a clear enthusiastic voice.
- Look directly at the interviewer when answering questions or asking a question.

Rule 12 – Be Positive

- Do not make negative comments about your current position, status, Military experience or co-workers.
- If you have been unemployed for an extended amount of time do not focus on it.

Rule 13 – Enthusiasm

- Show *enthusiasm* for the job.
- Tell the interviewer you are excited about the company and career opportunity.

Rule 14 – Show You Want the Job

- Show initiative, give examples of your ability to be a leader, team player, work independently, solve problems, and perform the job.

Rule 15 – Close the Interview

- Close the interview by asking the interviewer if they have any concerns about your ability to perform the job.
- Overcome any objections and *Ask For The Job™*.
- Wait for a response, thank the interviewer and ask about the next step in the interview process.

Rule 16 – Be Natural

- Be calm and natural during the interview closings.

Rule 17 – Thank You Letter

- After the interview email a *formal* thank you letter within twenty-four hours.
- You may email your thank you letter, however you should mail the hard copy.
- Thank each interviewer in a separate letter for taking time to meet with you.
- Make sure you have the correct spelling of their names and titles.
- In your thank you letter, identify two to four points the interviewer liked in bullet format.
- Use *spelling* and *grammar* check, and *re-read* your letter before mailing.

Rule 18 – Follow Up

- Contact your interviewer within one week unless otherwise instructed as to your interview status.

30 Powerful Civilian Interview Questions

INTRODUCTION

Interview preparation requires a successful strategy to obtain an offer for a new career opportunity in the civilian job market. Preparation starts with the candidate researching the organization and identifying the company mission, goals, products, services, customers, locations and competitors.

Are you prepared for your next interview?

Whether you have a telephone screening interview or one in person, preparation is essential to moving forward in the interview process.

Do you ask interview questions?

Candidates who prepare quality questions will be remembered. Often candidates ask few or no questions about the job. A lack of questions signals the interviewer you have given little or no thought about the position.

Why you should interact with the interviewer

Do you interact with the interviewer? Interviewers who do all the talking have no opportunity to assess your skills and strengths. Take control of the interview by responding to questions with "examples" of your achievements. People in general remember short stories. "Paint a Picture" by communicating your ability to perform the job based on past achievements.

Example. In the Military as a *(name of position)* I *consolidated* weekly and monthly reports for equipment inventory which allowed more time to perform other assignments. Note: "consolidated" is a key word

Example. In the Military as a *(name of position)* I *reduced* the time it took to repair equipment by... (tell how) which resulted in equipment being available in a timely manner to perform Military exercises. Note: "reduced" is a key word.

Why Should I Hire You?

Your goal in closing the interview is to answer the question in the hiring managers mind "Why Should I Hire You"? Asking quality interview questions engages the interviewer; providing examples of your skills sets you apart from the competition thereby positioning you as a candidate of choice.

Ask interview questions and gather valuable information.

There are many questions you should ask during an interview. Your goal is to gather valuable information you need to determine if this position is a good career move for your future.

Although you may not think to ask every question about the position, asking important questions about your role is essential in making an employment decision. Often candidates are not called back for a second interview - they have shown no interest in the position other than wanting or needing employment. Listed are questions to prepare you for your interview.

30 Powerful Civilian Interview Questions

1. Skills

- Where do you see my Military transferable skills in this position?

2. Changes

- What changes, if any would you like to see implemented in this position?

3. Goals

- What goals do you have for this position and how can my knowledge, skills and abilities help you achieve them?

4. Management

- To whom would I directly report to in this position?
- Would I be reporting to more than one person? If so, whom?

5. Leadership

- What type of leadership and personality are you looking for to fill this position?

6. Expectations

- What expectations do you have for this position in my first 90 days?

7. Team workers

- With whom will I be closely working with on a daily basis?

8. Core competency skills

- What specific core competency skills do I have that are of value to you and XYZ Corporation?

9. Challenges

- Are there any immediate challenges I will need to address in my first 90 days?

10. Projects

- Are there any pending projects that I should give priority to?

11. Business tools

- Will there be a laptop computer, cell phone, and other business tools available to me in this position?

12. Home office

- In this position, will I have the flexibility to work at or from my home office?

13. Employees

- How many employees would be reporting to me?
- Are all employees in good standing with the company?

14. Business reports

- What types of weekly, monthly, or quarterly reports will be required?

15. Overcome concerns

- Do you have any questions or concerns about my ability to successfully perform this position that I can address for you today?

16. Customer relationship management

- Is there an existing customer relationship management database?

17. Sales calls

- How many sales calls will I be required to make daily in my assigned territory?

18. Sales cycle

- Does this product or service have a long or short sales cycle?

19. New sales territory

- Why has this new sales territory been created?
- What are the cities or states for this territory?

- Will there be any overnight travel for this territory? If so, how often?
- Will I be required to provide storage for marketing materials?
- Will I be able to expense the storage if a use a storage facility?

20. Incentive program

- Is there a written bonus or commission program for this position?
- If so, when will I qualify for the program and how often is it paid?
- Does the incentive or bonus program change yearly?

21. Outside interview consultant

- Does XYZ Company hire outside consultants to screen candidates as part of the hiring process?

22. Executive telephone interviews

- May I have your email address to contact you if I have questions?

23. Employee benefits

- What is the effective date of employee benefits once I am hired?

24. New hire training

- What type of training is available for this position?

- How long and at what location?

25. Revenue

- How much revenue will I be accountable and responsible for in my sales territory, division or department?

26. Weekends

- Will I be required to work weekends for promotional events? If so, how often?

27. Credit Card

- Is there a corporate credit card for expenses?
- Will I be required to use my personal credit card for company expenses?
- How often are expenses reimbursed – weekly, bi-weekly or monthly?

28. Professional development – continuous learning

- Is there an internal university training program available for professional development?

29. Close – Ask For The Job™

- I'm excited about this position and the opportunity to use the skills you identified will be of value to XYZ Corporation. *May I please have the job?* Or, *May I please have this career opportunity?*
- Silence. Remain silent until the interviewer responds to your question. Silence is powerful.

30. Close – the next step

- What is the next step in the interview process?
- Will I have another opportunity to discuss my skills in more detail?

Interview Closing

- **Business Card** – Ask the interviewer for their business card.
- **Thank You** – Thank the interviewer for their time.
- **Thank You Letter** – Restate your skills in bullet format identified during the interview that will be valuable to the employer.
- **Email Thank You's** – Send an email thank you letter on your letterhead within 24 hours and mail the original copy to your contact.
- **Contact Works from Home Office** – If your contact works from home office and the address is not available, email your *formal* thank you letter in an attached word document using the company's headquarters or local office inside address.
- **Follow-up** – If you do not hear from your contact in the time they informed you, call or send an email of your continued interest in the position.
- **No Replies** – If you do not hear from your interview contacts after three attempts move on to another career opportunity.
- **New Opportunities** – *Always* have multiple career opportunities in the pipeline. Do not limit yourself to one position.

Business Dining Etiquette for the 21st Century

INTRODUCTION

Everyday a business meal is used for breakfast, lunch, teatime, and dinner. Professionals use business meals for interviews, performance reviews, promotions, meetings, conferences, meeting clients, presenting products and services, networking and other reasons.

What do your table manners say to others about you?

Table manners play an important role in making a positive impression in the business. Visible signs of your manners are essential to your professional success. Your social skills are on display; never assume others will not notice or be understanding of poor table manners. Polished table manners speak volumes about your professionalism, and can take your career or business to another level.

Business Dining Etiquette

Napkin Use

- Place your unfolded napkin on your lap.
- The napkin remains on your lap during the entire meal.

- Use your napkin to gently blot your mouth during your meal.
- At the end of the meal, place your napkin to the right of your dinner plate.
- Do not refold or bundle up your napkin.

Ordering

- Ask your server questions you might have about the menu.
- As a guest, do not order one of the most expensive items on the menu.
- Women's orders are usually taken before men's.
- Your server will determine how to take your order.

The Pre-Set Table Setting

As a general rule, liquids are on your right side and solids are on your left.

To the right

- Glassware
- Cup and saucer
- Knives and spoons
- Seafood fork, if seafood is included in the meal

To the left

- Bread and butter plate
- Small butter knife is placed horizontally across the top of the plate

- Salad plate
- Napkin and forks

Use of silverware

- The rule of silverware usage is work your silverware from the outside in.
- Use one utensil for each course.
- The salad fork is on the outer left, followed by your dinner fork.
- Your soup spoon is on your outer right, followed by your dinner knife.
- Dessert spoon and fork are placed above your plate or brought out with the dessert.

American vs. European Style

American style

- Cut food by holding your knife in the right hand and the fork in the left hand.
- Change your fork from your left hand to your right hand to eat, with the fork tines facing down.
- If you are left-handed, keep your fork in your left hand, tines facing up.

European (or Continental) style

- Cut food by holding your knife in your right hand while securing your food with your fork in your left hand.
- Your fork remains in your left hand, tines facing down.

- Your knife is in your right hand.
- Eat small pieces of food.
- Pick food up with your fork, which is in your left hand.

When you have finished your meal

- Do not push your plate away from you.
- Lay your fork and knife diagonally across your plate.
- Place your knife and fork side by side with the sharp side of the blade facing inward. The fork tines should face down. The knife and fork should be positioned at 10 and 4 o'clock.
- Do not place used silverware back on the table. Place it on the saucer. Unused silverware should be left on the table.
- Leave a soup spoon on your soup plate.

Business Table Manners

- **Doggy bag:** Do not ask for a doggy bag if you are a guest. Reserve doggy bags for informal dining.
- **Finger foods:** Finger foods can be messy and are best left for informal dining. Order foods that can be eaten with a knife and fork.
- **Alcoholic beverages:** Use good judgment. Behavior patterns tend to change when you drink. If you are employed, drinking during business hours is not recommended. Use good judgment.
- **Smoking:** Do not smoke while dining out; this might offend your guest. People form opinions

of you based on what they see and smell. Keep in mind some organizations are smoke free.

- **Body language:** Do not slouch; sit up straight at the table.

- **Resting your hands:** When you are not eating, keep your hands in your lap or resting on the table, with your wrists on the edge of the table. Elbows on the table are acceptable between courses but not during meals.

- **Food Seasoning:** Do not season your food before you have tasted it.

- **Chewing:** Never chew with your mouth open or make noises when you eat. Do not talk with your mouth full.

- **Slurping your soup:** Do not slurp your soup from the spoon or pick the bowl up to your mouth. Spoon your soup away from you when you take it out of the bowl. Do not blow your soup if it's hot; wait for it to cool.

- **Food between your teeth:** If you cannot remove the food between your teeth with your tongue, excuse yourself from the table and go to the rest room where you can remove the food in private. Those foods might include broccoli, spinach, fresh ground pepper, seeds, cereals or corn on the cob.

- **Eating bread and rolls:** Tear and butter one piece at a time.

- **Conversation:** Engage in lively conversation free of controversial topics such as politics, race, religion, or sex.

- **Leaving the table:** If you leave the table during the meal, simply excuse yourself.

- **Out of your reach:** If you need something on the table that is out of your reach, politely ask the person closest to the item to pass it to you.

- **Fallen silverware:** If a piece of silverware falls on the floor pick it up if you can reach it. Politely ask the server to bring you a replacement.

- **Food and liquid spills:** If food spills off your plate, pick it up with a piece of your silverware and place it on the edge of your plate. If a liquid spills, clean it up as much as you can, and limit the attention you draw to yourself.

- **Bad food:** Never spit out a piece of bad food or gristle into your napkin. Discreetly remove the food from your mouth with your utensil and place it on the edge of your plate. You may choose to cover it up with other food on your plate.

- **Dry mouth:** Keep your mouth moist. A dry mouth can cause white saliva deposits to appear on your lips, and in the corners of your mouth without your knowledge.

Power Career Fairs Making Connections Face to Face

INTRODUCTION

Career and job fairs are integral in your job search strategy and one of the most effective ways to land your dream job. You have the opportunity to market your skills to dozens of employers at one location.

Did you wear a business suit?

In a fair–like atmosphere it's essential you take the event seriously and make a powerful first impression just as you would in an employer's office. In a competitive environment do not underestimate the importance of your business image, behavior, body language, manners and overall professionalism.

Employers attend career fairs to find qualified candidates who have a positive attitude, are prepared, shows initiative and a sincere interest in working for their organization. Be ready to promote yourself and sell your skills on the spot. Tell employers about your strengths, achievements and why they should hire you.

What type of job are you looking for?

Knowing what you want shows you have done your home work. Research your targeted companies that will attend the career fair to identify which positions would be a match for your skills and experience. Make a primary and secondary target list of employers and spend *quality time* specifically marketing your skills to those employers. Collect business cards from employer representatives with whom you discuss career opportunities. Within 24 hours send an email or written thank-you letter to each of them.

There will be hundreds of job seekers who are marketing their skills just as you are. Set yourself apart by leaving a favorable and lasting impression in the minds of employers. Be kind and engaging to everyone you meet and make the most of your time at each employer booth.

Preparing For A Civilian Career Fair

In a competitive global market having the knowledge and skill to market your abilities is crucial in landing a new career opportunity. A fair event is the place to show you are serious and interested in gaining employment with a potential employer.

The guidelines will prepare you with strategies and tips to manage a career fair. Job seekers who are most successful at career fairs are those who prepare. Before attending a career fair, it is essential to know how to plan, execute and follow-up after the career fair.

Three Smart Preparation Strategies

1. **Plan** your career fair strategy

2. **Execute** your career fair strategy

3. **Follow-up** after your career fair

Plan Your Civilian Career Fair Strategy

Business Image

Do you wear casual attire to career fairs?

Your face-to-face contact with a potential employer is your "first interview" whether you have an appointment or not. *Casual attire is inappropriate and communicates you are not serious about your career.* The fact that you will only spend a few minutes at each employer's booth does not lessen the importance of your image.

Many employers have criteria when they meet with you – image is at the top of the list. Employers may note on your resume or application your "first impression" did not meet their expectations. If you ever wondered why you were not contacted after an interview perhaps your image excluded you from the hiring process.

- Plan to wear a "business suit" to make a positive first impression.
- Do not wear casual attire to the career fair – this could be a career limiting move.
- Your accessories, personal grooming and cleanliness should be impressive.
- Do not wear perfume or cologne.
- Make sure your teeth are clean with fresh breath.

Resume

- Always bring adequate copies of your resume printed on resume paper to work the career fair.
- Proofread your resume so there are no errors.

Reference List

- Have a list of your references prepared as part of your career portfolio.

- Provide contact information such as; contact name, title, company name, address, direct telephone number or extension, email address and if your reference is professional or personal contact.

- Indicate if your reference prefers phone or email contact. An example has been prepared for you.

Professional Reference Contact Information

Company Name

Contact Name

Contact Title

1234 Career Way

Career, CA 12345

Email address (Preferred)

Telephone Number

Cell Phone (Optional)

(Professional Reference)

Written References

- Include letters of achievements from Military service, civilian employment, volunteer and community work in your portfolio.

- References written on *letterhead* are most impressive.

Research

- Research companies you have an interview appointment with and those on your target list.

Prepare your 30-Second Commercial, Marketing or Sales Pitch

- Prepare and practice your 30 second commercial to promote and sell yourself.
- When an interviewer asks – "tell me about yourself" know what you plan to say.

Writing Tablet, Pen and Calendar

- Take a writing tablet of white paper in a leather portfolio to take notes after the interview or write down follow-up information.
- Use a quality name brand ink-pen with black ink for business.
- Do not use a pencil – it is a casual accessory and takes away from your business image.
- Take your personal calendar and be prepared to schedule a second interview on the spot.

Prepare Questions

- Be prepared with intelligent uncommon questions to ask the interviewer.
- Practice out loud your responses to interview questions you might be asked.
- Do not ask questions you could obtain answers to by going to the company website.

Location

- Know the exact location of the career fair and the parking situation including parking fees.

Be On Time!

- If you have a scheduled interview be on time and arrive 20 minutes prior to your interview time.

Program Floor Plan

- Study the floor plan so you will know where your interview or company targets are located.

Execute Your Civilian Career Fair Strategy

Resume Presentation

- Carry copies of your resume and references in a professional portfolio.
- Volunteer your resume – don't wait for the interviewer to ask for it.

Respect Everyone

- Treat every person you encounter with courtesy and respect. Employers do solicit input from other team members during hiring decisions.

Handshake

- Greet your interviewer with a confident handshake and sincere smile.

Listen

- Listen to the correct pronunciation of your interviewer's name and title.
- Listen to information about positions that might be of interest to you.

Title

- Address your interviewer by title (Ms, Mr., and Dr.) and last name unless invited differently.

Business Card

- Ask your contacts for their business cards.
- Use the contact information to email a thank-you letter and mail the original copy after the event.

Eye Contact

- Maintain good eye contact during your interview.

Sitting

- Take a seat only if you are invited to do so.
- Be still in your seat and avoid crossing your leg over your thigh. Crossing your leg over your thigh is considered "power" body language.
- Place your feet flat on the floor or cross them at your ankles to be more comfortable.

Interviewer Questions

- Respond to questions and provide examples of your achievements.

- A "short story" about your achievements helps the interviewer remember you and see you in the position.

Clarification

- Ask for clarification if you do not understand a question or procedure.

Thorough Responses

- Be honest, thorough and concise in your responses.

Be Yourself

- Do not "over-sell" your skills – you want a good career match between you and your employer.

Be Serious

- Treat the interview seriously and show the interviewer you are sincere about the career opportunity.

Be Positive

- Show a positive upbeat enthusiastic attitude.

Win-Win

- Evaluate the interviewer and organization. The goal is for a win-win outcome.
- Think about how you are treated and conduct yourself professionally.

Close – Ask For The Job™

- Practice "asking for the job" in your own environment so you will feel confident and comfortable expressing what you want – the job offer.

- If you are seriously interested in the career opportunity close – Ask For The Job™.

- You can do this by simply and confidently – not being arrogant use one of these closing strategies – *"May I please have this career opportunity?"* or *"May I please have the job?"* or *"May I please move to the next step in the interview process?"*

- It's not what you say when you ask for the job, it's *how you say it* that counts.

- Once you ask for the job – remain silent until the interviewer responds.

- The goal in "closing" the interview is to ask for what you want – the job offer.

- Asking an employer for the job is "promoting" or "selling" you. This unique strategy can position you for a second interview and a job offer.

Interview Process

- Ask the employer about the interview process, when and from whom you can expect to hear from them.

- Identify what action you are expected to take in the interview process.

Interview Close

- When the interviewer closes the interview, give a firm handshake, make positive eye contact and smile.
- Thank the interviewer for their time and company materials they have given you.

Interview Don'ts During The Career Fair

Attitude

- Don't exhibit a negative attitude during an interview. Stay positive and the job search process will have its rewards.

Body Language

- Don't slouch, sit on the edge of your chair or act anxious. Be aware and in control of your non-verbal body language.

Cell Phone

- TURN IT OFF!
- Don't take your cell phone with you during an interview if you travel by vehicle – leave it in your car.
- Don't underestimate the power of your first impression if your cell phone goes off during an interview.
- Don't have a cell phone ear-piece in your ear.
- Don't take a cell phone call if you forget to turn off your phone; turn off your phone, apologize and continue with your interview.

- Don't use a cell phone while you are walking around to employer booths; you are being observed. If you need to use your cell phone, leave the room of the career fair event.

Children, Friends, Parents, Pets or Spouse

- Don't take your children, friends, parents, pets or spouse with you. An assistance animal is not considered a pet.

Desperate

- Don't appear to be desperate for employment; don't appear to take any job offered.

False Information

- Don't falsify information on your application documents or interview questions.

Geographic Location

- Don't give the impression you are only interested in a specific location.
- Don't limit your geographic location.
- Be open to a reasonable location to get your foot in the door and prove your value.

Gum, Mints or Smell like Smoke

- Don't chew gum or suck mints.
- Don't smell like smoke. Smelling like smoke will be a turn-off to a new employer – especially one who does not smoke or a smoke free company.

- Don't have anything in your mouth including a ring piercing.

Interviewer's Questions

- Don't be unprepared for common interview questions about your background.
- A lack of preparation could eliminate you from the selection process.

Know What You Want

- Don't expect the interviewer to know what type of work you are interested in; do your research to identify the best position for your skills and experience.

Negative Comments

- Don't make negative comments or remarks about your difficulty finding employment, Military experience or your unemployment status.

Practice

- Don't use the interview as practice for another position.
- Don't treat your interview opportunity casually.

Salary

- Don't ask questions about or give the impression you are only interested in salary.
- Don't ask about company benefits or other perks until the subject is discussed with you by your interviewer.

- Never discuss how much money you receive from your Military retirement. Employers may use this information to pay you less than what you are worth. Keep this information confidential.

Follow Up After The Civilian Career Fair

Take Notes

- After each interview with an employer, take notes so you will not forget key points mentioned during your meeting.
- Do not take notes during your interview unless instructed to take down follow-up information.

Thank-You Letter

- Type your thank-you letter and email it within 24 hours.
- Use the thank-you letter to restate those key skills – in *bullet format* they liked about your background.

Follow-Up

- Follow-up when you are instructed to do so.
- Lack of follow-up skills can be the difference between achieving the next step in the interview process or a missed career opportunity.

Ten Civilian Career Fair Quick Tips

Career Fairs are excellent places to meet with employers, attend seminars, network and land a new career. Make the most of your time marketing your skills and selling yourself to employers so you will achieve your career goals.

1. Prepare to Interview

- Be prepared to interview on the spot.
- Quickly and effectively sell your skills, talents, experiences and yourself.
- Have a salary figure in mind in case the topic comes up. *Always* ask what the salary range is *before* you state your requirements.
- Once you know what the salary range is let your interviewer know in a very nice way it is open to negotiation. For example: "Thank you for providing the salary range, I'm excited about this position an open to negotiation."
- If there is a flat salary amount and no range for the position let the employer know if you will accept the amount they stated. Be prepared to make a decision on the spot if you will accept the salary stated.

2. Research

- Visit targeted employer's websites.
- Read business articles, financial reports, and other valuable information so you will "stand out" from your competitors.

3. Resumes

- Take at least 100 resumes on quality resume paper.
- Organize your personal information in a brief case or portfolio.
- Do not use a *backpack* or *book bag*.

4. Job Application

- Be proactive – complete an application on the employer's website and bring a copy with you.
- Your competition will have the advantage if they have a copy of their online application and you do not.
- Be prepared to neatly fill out an application on the spot in black ink if requested.
- Take your employment history dates and reference information with you.

5. Arrive Early

- Arrive 20 minutes early if you have a scheduled interview appointment.
- Arrive 30 minutes early to register and plan your career fair strategy.
- Review an employer booth floor plan if one is available.

6. Targeted Employers

- Visit your targeted employers first.
- Market your skills to other employers.

7. Collect Business Cards

- Collect business cards from each employer you meet.
- Email a thank-you letter to your contacts within 24 hours.

8. Take Notes

- Take notes after you speak with each employer while the information is fresh in your mind.

9. Closing the Interview – What is the next step?

- When closing the interview with an employer ask what is the next step in the interview process.
- If an employer informs you they will contact you – ask for permission to contact them if you have not heard from them within a specific time.

10. Visit Websites of Targeted Employers

- Visit websites of targeted employers that are of interest to you.
- Post your resume and complete an application online if you have not done so.

Seven Civilian Career Fair Bonus Tips

1. Personal Business Card

- Take your personal business cards with you for networking.

- Have a professional email address on your contact information.

2. Seminars and Networking

- Attend seminars and networking gatherings after you have met with your targeted employers.

3. Do Not Drink Alcoholic Beverages

- Network at casual gatherings but do not drink alcoholic beverages – your next employer might be observing you.

4. Interviewers Time

- Don't monopolize the interviewer's time. Be sensitive to others standing in line behind you.

5. Stand Alone

- Do stand alone and be independent of others.
- Be aware some employer's interview in groups.

6. Negative Words

- Avoid negative words like – "I can't", "I'm not", or "I won't".

7. Conversation Etiquette

- Don't invite yourself into a conversation an interviewer is having with another job seeker. Patiently wait for your turn to speak

Summary

The most important skills employers seek are *communication- interpersonal skills, adaptability-flexibility, problem-solving, teamwork, leadership-management skills, planning-organizing* and *willingness to learn* and *grow in your new position.* During every interview with civilian employers provide "examples" how your Military experience and skills are transferable to the civilian job market.

Civilian career fairs provide a valuable resource and benefits for you to explore careers and seek employment options.

Career Fairs enable you to:

- Market your skills to multiple industries.
- Gain valuable interview experience and advice from industry experts.
- Find out about key positions and submit your resume and application in person.
- Identify internships, research experiences and volunteer opportunities.
- Develop a network of new contacts.

Know what skills you have to offer and show employers the one asset they can't do without is YOU!

1. _____

2. _____

3. _____

4. _____

5. _____

6. _____

7. _____

8. _____

9. _____

10. _____

The Hidden Job Market
Four Steps for Success

INTRODUCTION

Job search has become a "contact" career strategy where you need contacts to land your next job. These contacts can be achieved by "internal" or "external" referrals – family, friends, Military contacts or associates that may work for a company or by contacting "targeted employers."

What is the Hidden Job Market?

The best jobs are never advertised on career websites, it's estimated about 20% of all jobs are *not* advertised to the public. These unadvertised jobs known as the "Hidden Job Market" are usually filled by referrals or by making direct contact with targeted employers. Employees who refer candidates save their organization time and money. Internal employees are given a monetary reward or other incentives to identify and refer qualified candidates. Listed are benefits of internal and external referrals and strategies to contact targeted employers.

Step 1: Employee Referral Benefits

- Employee referrals provide candidates with

distinct benefits compared to submitting a resume to a company on career websites.

Direct Contact

- Eliminates the possibility of your resume not being seen by the hiring manager.

Face-to-Face

- A phone call with the hiring manager positions you for a face-to-face meeting.

Sell Yourself

- You can sell *yourself, your knowledge, skills, abilities* and *enthusiasm* about the career opportunity.

Ahead of the Competition

- You will be several steps ahead of your competition and increase your chances of "closing" the career opportunity and landing your dream job.

Step 2: External Referral Benefits

- Contacts you may know or meet may have a referral for you at your targeted company.
- Being referred by someone who worked for or knows someone at your targeted company can open the door for you.

Step 3: How to Contact Targeted Employer's

- To begin any job search you should identify your "selling points" to a potential employer.

- Target a position, industry and list of companies that are a good match with your skills.
- Next, learn about the "employers" needs and contact the company for an interview. Although this process is easy, preparation and follow-up are the keys to achieving direct contact and a successful outcome. Listed are strategies to prepare you for your job search.

Title of Position

- Identify the title of the position of interest. You might need to call the company, explain your interest and find out the title of the position. Although some titles vary for different companies the job description may be similar.

Key Contact

- Identify who is the key contact, title, email address and phone number or extension of your contact. You may also consider checking the company website organizational chart for key contact information.
- Use the internet to find a person of interest. Once you know the persons name search them on one or more social websites. This technique will provide you with valuable background information about your contact.

Telephone Script

Prepare a telephone script of what you will say to your key contact. You may want to practice before you call a hiring manager. An easy script has been created to help you get started.

- Hello my name is…
- I was referred to you by…or
- I'm calling to confirm you are the hiring manager for a…position
- I have a background of Military experience in…
- I'm interested in a career in … and wondered if you would be open to meeting with me to discuss career opportunities at XYZ Company.
- Would your calendar be available…..or…..?

If you have spoken with your decision maker ask for their email address to send your resume and cover letter. In addition, mail your resume and portfolio to your contact prior to your appointment date. This strategy allows your contact to review your background prior to your meeting, prepare questions and mentally start to see you in the position.

If you have not spoken with a decision maker but have their contact information, mail your resume and portfolio to them. In your cover letter indicate when you will follow-up with them to schedule an appointment for an introduction.

These effective strategies improve your chances of meeting with a targeted employer and show your professionalism.

Step 4: The "Gatekeeper"

Although the process may seem easy you might encounter "gatekeepers", these are the administrative professionals whose job is to screen the phone calls and keep you away from the decision makers. To get past the gatekeepers you might consider these strategies.

- Call early at 7:45 or 8:45
- Call after business at 5:05
- If you know the phone extension of your decision maker they may pick-up. *Many professionals arrive early and stay late. Be prepared if your contact takes your call.*
- If you do not have a phone extension of your contact, try calling during lunch time when the regular administrative professional goes to lunch. Another person may be more open to providing you with contact information.
- When you call a company you improve your chances of getting what you want when you make brief small talk, are courteous, professional and say please and thank-you.

Summary

The goal in identifying positions in the *"hidden job market"* is to be connected directly to the hiring manager either by an internal or external referral or by contact information you obtain by calling the targeted company. Be sure to follow-up with all referrals and provide feedback to people who have assisted you with your job search.

When your contact efforts lead you to meetings with a hiring manager you can demonstrate your *interest, expertise,* and *enthusiasm* you have for the position. The hidden job market strategy will position you several steps ahead of other candidates and closer to landing you a new career opportunity.

Recruit your Past Managers

INTRODUCTION

Are you looking for a job? Looking for employment is one of the most personal and challenging experiences a professional will face during their career. If you are looking for a job you have an opportunity to start your own business or consider employment in a new field until a position opens up in your desired industry. Transferable skills can be used in multiple industries.

Consider every job you have had – Military service, a volunteer, internships, community work, part or full time employment regardless whether you were paid or not. For every position you had, someone hired you – now it's time to "recruit your past managers" to assist you in your job search. Listed are strategies you can use to recruit them.

Make a List

- Make a list of all of your past managers from the Military, employment, volunteer and community work positions.

Internet Search

- Use "social networking" websites to search for

contacts. With some basic knowledge such as the full name you can easily find them.

Where Are They?

- Many people list their employment in their personal profile, what type of work they do and where they are now. Contacting them could possibly open the door for a new career.

Make Contact

- Contact the company where they are employed and ask to speak with them.

Refresh their Memory of Who You Are

- Refresh their memory of who you are and where they hired you. Chances are they will remember you and be glad to help you in your job search.
- Always ask if this is a good time to talk, some people may not be as responsive if they are in a middle of a project.

Employment Status

- Inform your contact of what type of work you are looking for and employment status – you may be unemployed or looking for a new career.

Ask for Help

- Ask for help regarding your job search at their place of employment including other divisions, departments or other companies.

Career Advice

- Be open and ask for career advice that could help you in your job search.

Referrals

- Ask for referrals to someone in their network. They may volunteer to help you by contacting someone on your behalf.

New Employment

- Use "recruit your past manager" strategy if you are in Military to Civilian Transition or looking for a new employment.

Follow-up Tips

- Outcome – Contact everyone your past managers referred you to and let them know of the outcome.
- Thank You – Send your past managers and everyone who assisted you in your job search a thank you note.
- Job Search Progress – Keep your past managers informed of your job search progress especially when you find employment.

No Response

- When you contact a past manager and initially they seem excited and want to help you then stop responding to your phone calls let it go. After a few phone calls to them with no response take the cue they are not going to call you back.

- Sometimes people feel obligated to help you but do not know how to tell you they can not assist you for whatever their reasons may be. Accept this as a learning experience and move on.

Keep in Touch

- Keeping in touch with past managers is a great strategy for employment and building relationships.
- When possible an annual breakfast, lunch or dinner would be appropriate to show you value their business relationship.
- During the holiday season sending a card shows your professionalism and willingness to stay in contact with them.

Interview Mental Preparation Strategies

INTRODUCTION

Whether you are a new or experienced civilian professional you should mentally prepare for your interview. Recall important Military facts, figures and other supportive information that will successfully move you through the interview process. Practice your responses so you can easily answer the interviewer's questions and tie your transferable skills to the job description. Listed are strategies to help you organize your thoughts.

Twelve Interview Strategies

1. Elevator Speech

- Practicing what you are going to say will help you remember key points.
- Avoid stumbling in your conversation and build self-confidence.

2. Contract Negotiations

- "I saved $2 million dollars in one year for the Military in my position as an equipment buyer by applying new negotiation skills I gained in a certification program."

3. Direct Mail Campaign

- "I launched a direct mail campaign that gave a 12 percent return rate on XYZ company investment of the project."

4. Facts

- "My manager supported new ideas I recommended that helped accomplish department goals, For example...."

5. Figures

- "I reduced equipment costs by $100,000 annually by identifying a similar product that was less expensive, more features and benefits than the existing product.

6. Industry Trends

- Be knowledgeable of the latest industry news and trends.

7. New Technology Launches

- "I led the personnel department in a successful launch of XYZ technology service used for... which resulted in..."

8. Percents

- "I reduced costs by 15 percent by researching and identify new vendors for office equipment on Military bases."

9. Savings

- "I reduced costs by $50,000 annually by eliminating a food service line that was not being used enough by the Military to justify the expense."

10. Stats

- "I improved...by... percent which resulted in...."

11. Research

- Company research
- Job description details
- Check the company website about information regarding the hiring manager.

12. Other

- Other information you feel will help position you as a candidate of choice.

Twelve Tools To Prepare For A Civilian Interview

INTRODUCTION

How do you prepare for your interview? Interview preparation is a significant step in your job search process. Candidates who are serious about their career should invest time they need to sell their top skills at every interview. Nothing less would be expected of a candidate who wants to get hired.

Twelve Tools to Prepare For A Civilian Interview

Tool 1: Preparation

- Preparation is essential to a successful interview and should begin three to five days prior to your scheduled interview.
- The time you spend pre-planning for the interview will improve your close ratio, help position you for a second interview and job offer.

Tool 2: Company Size

- How large is the company in terms of assets, locations, and employees? This will help you establish company stability and promotional opportunities.

Tool 3: Established Date

- The date establishes the company reputation although no guarantee for job security.

Tool 4: Mission and Vision Statements

- These statements provide a discussion about organizational goals, how your skills can be of value.
- Provide an example of a short memorable story by "painting a picture" of your achievements that will be beneficial to your interview success.

Tool 5: Products and Services

- Prepare questions that relates to the company's products and services.
- Many interviewers will ask you – What do you know about XYZ company? This is where your knowledge about what they do will be valuable. If you reply with a general response such as "I know you are a big company" you will be seen as unprepared and not knowledgeable about what they do and possibly screened out of the interview process.
- Respond to the interviewer with detailed information that shows you have done your homework and how your transferable skills will be an asset to their organization.

Tool 6: Target Market and Competitors

- Know where the company target markets are and competitors in those markets.

- Ask a question about the company's goals for new markets and products. You might find this information on the website.
- Ask a question such as "Do you have a target date to launch ABC product I saw on the website"?
- Your knowledge about the company's products or services can create dialogue, which can position you for the next step in the interview process.

Tool 7: Strategic Goals and Plans

- Create interview questions based on the company goals and plans. An interview question you might ask is: "How can I help you achieve the departmental goals"?
- Your goal is to have the interviewer describe what they like about your background and how they see you in the position.

Tool 8: What's New – Events, New Developments and any Special Projects?

- Discuss events or projects and how your experience has provided you with the skills to take a leadership role in current or future projects.

Tool 9: Financial Status

Are they hiring or downsizing, closing divisions or improving them, adding new products or services?

- Your knowledge of the company finances will impact your career decision. These questions and others will provide insight as to whether this is the place for you.

Tool 10: Organizational Chart

- The organizational chart will indicate who the key employees are and where advancement opportunities would be.

Tool 11: Social Responsibility

- What community initiatives does the company participate in and how does it fit with your interests.
- Refer to the company initiatives during your interview and express your interest if they are similar.

Tool 12: Industry Issues

- Read industry periodicals about upcoming changes that will impact the company and how your skills can be beneficial.

Job Search Civilian Interview Checklist

INTRODUCTION

To prepare for your interview a checklist will assist you in ensuring you are organized. Listed are steps to help you get started.

Fourteen Steps to Prepare for Your Civilian Interview

1. **Clean your briefcase or portfolio.** Remove all documents that are not relevant to your interview.

2. **Company information.** Be sure to have the full name, title, department and telephone number of the person you will be meeting.

3. **Business Address.** Get the complete address, building, suite number, and parking information where your interview is scheduled.

4. **Directions.** Do an internet search, ask for directions or use a device that will provide directions for your interview. Allow pre-interview time to take a trial drive to the location during low traffic patterns to allow for unforeseen circumstances such as construction delays. Knowing where you are going on your interview day gives you peace of mind.

5. **Resume.** Bring a minimum of three copies of your resume to the interview. Although the company

may already have a copy this shows professionalism, and how well you are prepared for more than one interviewer. Companies often times will ask you for a copy of your resume even though they have a copy to see if you are prepared.

6. **Letters of reference.** Include letters of reference preferably on letterhead paper. References written on letterhead paper give more credibility to the document.

7. **Presentation of resume and references.** Purchase a professional portfolio to place your resume, cover letter, references and other achievements. The portfolio should have a place for you to place your personal business card on the *outside* of the folder.

8. **Personal business card.** Have your personal business cards made with your contact information and professional email address. You may need to create a professional email for your job search. Do not use business cards that have "free" and the printers name on the reverse side. Pay extra for business cards and perhaps use the reverse side to have your own personal career slogan or tagline related to your industry or leave it blank. Computer generated business cards provide another option however be sure to keep it professional and maintain your image.

9. **Executive pen.** Purchase an executive pen or pen and pencil set. Having your name engraved adds a personal touch and will not go un-noticed.

10. **Leather writing portfolio.** Bring a leather writing portfolio in black or dark brown with white writing paper, yellow paper if you are in the legal or financial industry. There should be a place in the portfolio for

you to place your business card and a place for those you collect from your interviewers.

11. **Attache or Portfolio type Bags.**

   - **Women.** Its recommended women use a soft style bag and not carry an attaché and purse. Place your identification information in your portfolio bag.
   - **Men.** Use a professional portfolio bag that is not oversized and easy to access your information.

12. **Company research.** Bring company research information with you to review in your car prior to your interview. There is no need for you to bring this information into your interview.

13. **Interview questions.** Prepare, write and remember five quality questions per interview. Only look at these questions if you forget your questions – ask for permission to look at your questions from your interviewer before you look.

14. **Interview image.** Plan your attire three to five days prior to your interview. This allows time for dry cleaning, or the unexpected. Shoes should be polished and in good condition.

Thirty One Top Civilian Interview Questions You May Be Asked

1. Tell me about yourself?

2. What are your strengths?

3. What are your weaknesses?

4. How would you describe your proudest career achievement?

5. How do you plan your work day?

6. Do you have any questions for me?

7. What salary are you seeking for this position?

8. Describe your responsibilities in your last position.

9. What do you know about XYZ Company?

10. How long will it take you to make a contribution to our bottom line?

11. Are you open to relocation for promotional opportunities?

12. What would you do to improve department performance in the first 90 days?

13. Do you have a personal mission statement?

14. What business tools do you use to keep yourself organized?

15. How have you spent your time during your unemployment?

16. What is your greatest achievement during your unemployment?

17. What is your greatest failure and what did you learn from it?

18. Why did you leave your last position?

19. Why are you looking for employment?

20. How well do you work in a team environment?

21. What do you know about this industry?

22. Would my casual attire make you feel uncomfortable when introducing me to customers?

23. Tell me about a problem you had and the steps you took to solve it?

24. Give me an example of when you had to deal with conflict on the job.

25. Describe your written and oral communication skills.

26. How do you manage your time?

27. How well do you work with diverse groups of people?

28. Give me an example of your listening skills.

29. Where would you like to be in your career three years from now?

30. Why should I hire you?

31. What was the last business book you read? What is the author's name? Why did you read this book? What was your take away?

   - If you have not read a business book in the last twelve months discuss a business article you have read. Provide the title, author, source of the article and your take away.

   - It's important to state you have read something business related rather than nothing.

Transferable Skills to Market to Civilian Employers

INTRODUCTION

What are key words and how should I use them in my interview? Key words also known as "power verbs" are listed in the employer's job description and should be included in your resume and cover letter. Key words show your accomplishments. Using key words during your interview conversation will reinforce your knowledge and achievements and provide the hiring manager with insight about your transferable skills.

Why Key Words are important

It's *imperative* you use key words in examples to identify your *knowledge, skills, abilities* and *experience*. The goal in providing examples differentiates you from other candidates and allows you to sell your strengths to the hiring manager. Listed are key words and categories to help you communicate your exceptional skills.

Ten Categories and Key Words to Use in your Resume and Cover Letter

COMMUNICATION

1. Communication

- Clarified
- Communicated
- Consulted
- Dedicated
- Demonstrated
- Educated
- Illustrated
- Informed
- Interviewed
- Negotiated
- Persuaded
- Questioned
- Reinforced
- Represented
- Substantiated
- Suggested
- Summarized
- Supported
- Tested
- Translated
- Verified

EXECUTING

2. Executing

- Administered
- Carried Out

- Completed
- Conducted
- Distributed
- Exercised
- Handled
- Installed
- Operated
- Performed
- Processed
- Produced
- Proved
- Shipped
- Sold
- Stocked
- Transacted

HELPING

3. Helping

- Advised
- Cooperated
- Counseled
- Elevated
- Enhanced
- Helped
- Mobilized
- Provided
- Protected
- Rehabilitated
- Relieved
- Rescued
- Served
- Sustained
- Validated

LEADERSHIP

4. Leadership

- Accelerated
- Directed
- Empowered
- Influenced
- Led
- Managed
- Mentored
- Motivated
- Promoted
- Set Goals
- Stimulated
- Strengthened
- Supervised
- Trained
- Transformed

ORGANIZING

5. Organizing

- Activated
- Adjusted
- Allocated
- Arranged
- Assigned
- Centralized
- Coordinated
- Delegated
- Designated

- Dispatched
- Established
- Facilitated
- Implemented
- Incorporated
- Issued
- Linked
- Mapped Out
- Obtained
- Ordered
- Organized
- Programmed
- Recruited
- Retrieved
- Routed
- Scheduled
- Secured
- Simplified
- Tracked

PLANNING

6. Planning

- Administered
- Anticipated
- Determined
- Developed
- Evaluated
- Forecasted
- Formulated
- Identified
- Planned

- Prepared
- Researched
- Revised
- Strategize

PROBLEM SOLVING

7. Problem Solving

- Analyzed
- Brainstormed
- Collaborated
- Created
- Debugged
- Decided
- Detected
- Diagnosed
- Engineered
- Formulated
- Investigated
- Recommended
- Remedied
- Repaired
- Revamped
- Revived
- Satisfied
- Solved

QUANTITATIVE

8. Quantitative

- Appraised
- Balanced
- Budgeted
- Calculated
- Compiled
- Computed
- Converted
- Dispersed
- Estimated
- Increased
- Multiplied
- Projected
- Purchased
- Quantified
- Recorded
- Reduced
- Tabulated
- Totaled

RESULTS

9. Results

- Accomplished
- Achieved
- Advanced
- Combined
- Consolidated
- Contributed

- Delivered
- Demonstrated
- Diminished
- Eliminated
- Enlisted
- Excelled
- Expanded
- Expedited
- Gained
- Generated
- Improved
- Increased
- Introduced
- Joined
- Launched
- Minimized
- Obtained
- Opened
- Overcame
- Produced
- Qualified
- Received
- Restored
- Targeted
- Uncovered

SUPERVISION

10. Supervision

- Analyzed
- Developed
- Established

- Inspected
- Maintained
- Measured
- Modified
- Policed
- Reviewed
- Revised
- Supervised
- Traced
- Updated

Fifteen Ways to Use Key Words in your Interview Conversation

1. Coordinated

- "I coordinated...meetings, events, projects, new recruits, new hire or training orientation."

2. Created

- "I created...a new or improved map, document, product, or procedure."

3. Developed

- "I developed...a new strategy, procedure, policy, or master schedule."

4. Forecasted

- "I forecasted...budgets, purchases, new equipment or troops needed."

5. Implemented

- "I implemented...a new strategy, plan or procedure."

6. Increased

- "I increased Military...supplies, communication, production or performance..."
- 'I increased the amount of troops in a certain region to prepare for...."

7. Leadership

- "I supervised a team of civilian and military personnel to accomplish a......mission....."

8. Managed

- "I managed...projects, Military staff and civilian personnel, new recruits, orientation..."

9. Organized

- "I organized...Military training, reports, and a dinner program, and conference, movement of equipment, vehicles or community event."

10. Planned

- "I planned a new strategy, procedure, plan for..."

11. Purchased

- "I purchased office supplies, uniforms, equipment, military vehicles or tools."

12. Reduced

- "I reduced...troops, costs, expenses, production or travel time."

13. Scheduled

- "I scheduled a.... transfer, increased or reduced.... or time needed to..."

14. Supervised

- "I supervised...Military staff, civilian employees, a procedure, projects, or new construction development."

15. Trained

- "I trained field personnel, new recruits, basic training...."

Top Ten Transferable Skills to Market to Civilian Employers

The key to getting hired is marketing your top transferable skills to civilian employers. Use the listed strategies to "stand out" from other candidates.

- **Skills** - Identify skills required for the job based on the job description.
- **Transferable Skills** - Identify top skills you have that are transferable to the civilian job market.
- **Provide Examples** - Provide examples of your top skills in a "short story" how you used them in the military and past employers.

- **Confirm** - Confirm how your transferable skills are a match for the career opportunity.
- **Overcome Objections** - Overcome objections by the employer with a plan of action to improve skills.

Top Ten transferable Skills

1. New Skills and Concepts

- Advanced training and concepts to apply in the civilian job market
- Learned and applied real world situations
- Enhance productivity in the workplace to achieve positive outcomes

2. Leadership Qualities

- Leadership by example
- Leadership through direction
- Leadership by delegation of assigned tasks
- Leadership, motivate and inspire
- Leadership to achieve desired results

3. Teams

- Works in teams or independently
- Responsible for teams goals
- Supports teams objectives and implementation
- Performs at high level independently
- Achieves independent goals

4. Interpersonal Skills

- Diversity – Works well with all cultural backgrounds

5. Works Efficiently and Diligently

- Time Management Skills
- Works with limited resources and achieves goals
- Achieves time management goals under pressure

6. Accountability

- Accountable for actions of self and subordinates
- Elevates issues through the proper chain of command

7. Technology and Globalization

- Trained to use cutting edge technology to achieve goals

8. Personal Integrity

- Abides by a strong Code of Ethics
- Security Clearances for sensitive information
- Proven track record of trustworthiness

9. Health and Safety Protocols

- Adheres to a drug-free workplace
- Respect for employees, materials, property and procedures

10. Triumph over Adversity

- Determination – Achieves goals when faced with adversity

Why Should I Hire You?

The Most Important Question

Your Resume Must Answer

INTRODUCTION

Why should I hire you? A well written and polished resume will get the attention of the hiring manager. Will your resume answer the question in the hiring manager's mind "Why should I hire you?"

Managers, human resources support staff, talent management and recruiters invest an enormous amount of time reviewing resumes. Their busy schedules leave little time for them to spend on each resume. In fact, many staff professionals spend 20 seconds or less on each resume they review. It makes good business sense for you to grab their attention quickly and motivate them to contact you.

Resume "Skill Benefit" or "Selling Statement"

Why are these statements important?

Hiring managers are looking for one element that makes you stand out from other candidates. To capture their attention you need a resume that has a strong "skill benefit statement."

When you add the skill benefit statement to your resume you will increase your chances of being interviewed, because the hiring manager will want to know more about you.

Grab attention early by placing your one sentence statement at the top of the first page, this is your "sales pitch" which the decision maker will read.

Here is an example of an unsuccessful "skill benefit" or "selling statement":

"Excellent oral and written communication skills."

Here is an example of a successful benefit statement you should write.

"Presented a new field training program for 200 recruits resulting in a 25 percent increase in retention over a 12 month period."

Your resume is a powerful "sales tool" to accomplish one goal – get you an interview. It should communicate a skill benefit statement and answer the question in the hiring manager's mind - "Why should I hire you"? When you write your resume consider these resume tips.

Twenty Three Smart Resume Tips

1. Contact Information

- Include your name, home address, telephone number and professional email address.
- Use a telephone number which you can speak freely.
- Do not use a work telephone number unless you are applying within your organization.

2. Proofread

- Do not proofread your own resume or rely only on spelling and grammar check.

- When you proofread your own writing you tend to "read" what you want to be there instead of what is actually written.

- Ask a mentor or friend who has good grammar skills to provide constructive feedback.

- You may consider setting your resume aside for a few hours – then re-read it out loud for corrections.

3. Detailed Work History

- Be specific about your work history and achievements that will motivate a hiring manager to call you for an interview.

- Eliminate information that will have no impact in gaining an interview.

4. Personal Pronouns

- Personal pronouns such as, "I", "me", "mine", and "our" should not be on your resume. Resumes are written in first person. For your job description instead of writing for example; "I managed a sales territory..." You would write "Managed a sales territory..."

5. Numerical Symbols

- Use numerical symbols instead of spelling out the number word. Numerical symbols stand out and create "eye spots" for the reader. For example:

"Developed a dynamic team of seven marketing professionals."

It would catch the reader's eye more quickly if you use a numerical symbol for example:

"Developed a dynamic team of 7 marketing professionals."

6. Show Case Your Achievements: Why Should I Hire You?

- Hiring managers want to see your achievements rather than a job description on your resume.
- How do you stand out from the crowd? What strategies did you use to reduce costs, work more efficiently, increase sales, solve problems, and what did you do to catch the eye of management or the officer in charge?
- Write your achievements in bullet format using action verbs.

7. Be Positive

- Include only those things in your resume that will attract an employer to you.
- Omit reasons for leaving a job and other career setbacks.
- Information that is not positive leave off.
- Use the application to document gaps of employment with volunteer work and internships.

8. Be Prepared

- Be prepared for unplanned telephone interviews by having your resume employment dates, salary history, reason for leaving and current employment status in a folder near each telephone you use.
- A cell phone is not recommended due to the chance your call could drop.
- If you choose to use a cell phone be sure to get the telephone number of the caller as soon as possible during the call.

9. Plain Text

- Do not use fancy fonts, use standard fonts only.

10. Resume Sections

- Use common resume sections such as contact information, skills, summary of experience, work experience, education, summary of qualifications, and finishing touches such as awards, memberships and certifications.

11. Paragraphs

- Do not write in paragraphs instead write *only* in bullet format.

12. Sell Yourself

- Sell yourself but do not exaggerate or oversell your skills.

13. Art work

- Avoid art work or pictures unless you are an actor, artist, model or in the fashion industry.

14. References

- Put references on a separate sheet of paper. Include your contact information in a letterhead format.

- There is no need to state on your resume "references available upon request." Always include references as part of your resume portfolio.

15. Resume Paper

- Use only standard 8.5 x 11 quality paper in white, off-white, or cream paper. Avoid using fancy colored paper.

16. Abbreviations

- Do not use abbreviations that are not well known to other industries where you might use transferable skills.

17. Format

- Balance your resume with information about your skill-set, achievements and employment history.

- For each position you had in the Military for the last ten years list the position, your title, location or ship name and dates.

18. Objective or Summary of Experience

- An "objective" should be included on the first page of your resume. Without an objective it will leave the reader wondering what position you are applying for and your career objective.

19. Personal Branding Statement

- You have about 20 seconds to make a first impression on paper. The personal branding statement will distinguish you from other candidates. This one sentence statement should say three things:
  1. Who you are
  2. Your most outstanding strengths
  3. The best value you bring to an employer

Example:

"Seasoned sales executive – builds strong relationships, exceptional presentations and closing skills which increased sales for my employer over $500,000 in annual sales."

Place your personal branding statement in "italics" on the first page of your resume below your contact information. A strong branding statement will distinguish you from other candidates with similar skills and catch the eye of the reader.

20. Keywords or Tags

- A resume without keywords is sure to be overlooked. Computer software programs are designed to flag resumes for keywords. A human reader will pre-qualify your resume by searching for skills to satisfy the job description.

21. On-Line Resumes

- Update your resume every 30 days on – online job search websites.
- Small changes in your skill set can bring about positive results.

22. Employment Gap

- Avoid becoming a victim of the employment gap. If you are unemployed immediately fill the gap on your resume with *documented* volunteer, self employment, community or internship work.
- Documentation will allow you to provide references for your work.
- The longer you are unemployed the *less* marketable you are in the eyes of potential employers and recruiters regardless of the economic climate.
- Employment gaps can *diminish* your opportunities to gain employment.
- Fill the gap and get hired

23. Soft and Hard Skills

- List both soft and hard skills on your resume based on the job description. A resume without both skills will limit your career opportunities.
- Soft skills are in-demand by employers; they are people related skills which are transferable from one industry to another.
- Hard skills are technical or job specific skills.

Summary

The goal of your resume is to "sell" not tell.

You only have a few seconds to capture the reader's eye and every second counts. The job market stakes are higher - employers are more selective about candidates they choose to join their company. A resume that lacks key elements can hold you back and put you in the rejection pile. Use these resume tips to encourage hiring managers to contact you and find out more about you.

STRATEGY FOURTEEN

Cover Letter Strategies

INTRODUCTION

What is the purpose of a cover letter? The cover letter is a powerful "marketing tool" used to create interest about your knowledge, skills and abilities and position you as a strong candidate for the career opportunity. A cover letter is a critical part of your job search strategy and should *not* be considered an option.

How does the cover letter help me?

A cover letter introduces you and sets the stage of what an employer can expect from you. This document should provide a compelling overview of your background, current employment status and why your transferable skills are the best match for the position and employer.

What does your "written impression" say about you?

The submission of your resume and cover letter online is the first "written impression" to an employer. You only have a few minutes to showcase your written communication skills and pass or fail screening by human resources or talent management staff.

The first few sentences should illustrate your achievements and knowledge about the company. Next explain how the company can benefit from your accomplishments. Market your skills by using knowledge about the company and your experience to create a reason in the employer's mind why they should interview you.

To be considered for a new career use cover letter tools to position you for a face-to-face interview.

Ten Cover Letter Career Tools

1. Mission and Vision Statements

- What information in the mission and vision statements does your accomplishments tie-in with your achievements and goals?

2. Organizational Goals

- What are the company's goals and how can your experience add value?

3. Press Releases

- How can your knowledge about the company's products and services open the door for you?

4. Community Relations

- What organizations does your company support and why? Do you have similar interests or contacts?

5. Professional Skills

- What professional and transferable skills do you have that will benefit your target company?

6. Training Seminars

- What training seminars or classes have you completed in the Military that could give you an advantage over other candidates? Are these training classes listed on your resume?

7. Certifications and Certificates

- What certifications and certificates do you have that will be valuable? Do you have copies to present during your interview?

8. Industry Changes

- What transferable skills do you have that can benefit the organization due to industry changes?

9. Industry Contacts

- What industry contacts do you have that will strengthen business relationships?

10. Products, Services, Contracts and Customers

- What specific knowledge do you have that could be a key asset to a new employer?

Before you write your cover letter consider these tips:

Seven Cover Letter Preparation Tips

1. Customize your Cover Letter

- Do not use a form or template cover letter.
- Customize your letter for each position you apply for.

2. Job Descriptions

- Review the job description in detail.

3. Key Words

- Identify key words in the job description you can use in your cover letter.

4. Create a List of Transferable Skills

- Create a list of your top transferable skills and how they parallel to the job description.

5. Strong Points

- Focus on the strong points of the job description but keep it short.

6. Salutation

- Call the company and get your contacts name. If you are unable to get a contact name, address the cover letter to: Dear Human Resources Manager,

Dear Recruiter, Dear Talent Management, Dear Vice President of Sales or Dear Project Director.

- Gender. If you can not determine the person's gender by their name use the person's first initial and last name; example: Samara Lee should be written:

Dear S. Lee:

Take the safe strategy rather than make a mistake that could cost you an interview.

- Do not use general inside salutations such as; To Whom It May Concern, Dear Sir, or Dear Madam. Your attention to detail improves your chance of being selected for an interview.

7. Proofread

- Do not rely on spell-check. Proofread and check your cover letter and resume for errors.

Four Cover Letter Rules

Rule 1 – Paragraph 1

- Identify the position for which you are applying.
- Match your letterhead to your resume letterhead.
- Create a one sentence "branding statement" that relates to your achievements in the industry.
- Center your statement in italics below your letterhead contact information. Place your name below the quote to show ownership. This

branding strategy captures the reader's attention and allows you to stand out from others.

- State where you learned about the position.
- Include the name of the position, location, city and state, reference identification number or job description number – this shows your attention to detail. Place this information below the company inside address. For example.

Date
XYZ Company
1234 Career Way
Career City, California 12345

Position: Project Manager
Job ID or Reference #: 23456
Location: US-CA – Career City, CA

Dear Talent Management:

Rule 2 – Paragraph 2

- This paragraph is the bridge that connects your qualifications to the position.
- The company website can be a valuable resource to organize your thoughts.
- Read the company website, job description and identify information you can use that will assist you in opening the door.

Rule 3 – The Closing Paragraph

- The last paragraph is your "closing pitch."
- Thank the reader for their time; ask to meet with them to discuss your qualifications in more detail.

Here is an example:

Option 1: Advertised Position

"I would appreciate an opportunity to meet with you to discuss my experience and background in more detail and how they may be of value to you and XYZ Company. I look forward to your reply."

Thank you for your time and consideration.

Option 2: Unadvertised Position – Hidden Job Market

"I would appreciate an opportunity to meet with you to discuss my experience and background and how they can be of value to you and XYZ Company. I will contact your office to schedule an appointment to meet you."

Thank you for your time and consideration.

Rule 4 – Follow-up

- Follow-up with your contact within three to five business days when you email the letter.
- Depending on your circumstance you may choose to email and mail the hard copy.
- Be persistent, it might take a few telephone calls to get your interview.
- Do not be surprised if your cover letter package has been forwarded to another person who will contact you – this is a good sign in the interview process.

- Be careful not to sound frustrated or desperate when you call or send a follow-up email.

- If you do not receive a response after three contact attempts consider a non-response as a *no* for this opportunity. *Always* have other alternatives.

Summary

The goal of a cover letter is to capture the attention of the hiring manager and position you for an interview. When you take the time to write a cover letter it shows your interest and desire for the position. A powerful cover letter will engage employers in what you have to offer and motivate them to invite you for an interview.

Your cover letter should be original – it will open or close the door based on how well it's written. This is an employer's first *written impression* of you and how well you communicate on paper. Employer's use cover letters as a screening strategy to evaluate your communication skills. A resume without a cover letter is not acceptable in any job market. If you have applied for jobs without a cover letter you possibly have eliminated yourself from the screening process.

A cover letter is the first step in the interview process and your door to a new career opportunity. Use these tools and tips to make you "stand out" from other candidates.

Effective Telephone Interviewing Skills

INTRODUCTION

Are you prepared for your civilian telephone interview? Employers increasingly rely on telephone interviews to screen candidates for employment. Candidates should be prepared for scheduled and unscheduled telephone calls. It's not enough for candidates to be available to discuss the career opportunity in person, but also comfortable speaking to executives on the telephone.

Why is a telephone interview important?

A telephone interview can be more important than the face-to-face – it's your first impression with a potential employer. Your telephone interview can be the deciding factor if you should move to the next step in the interview process. Usually a telephone interview lasts approximately 20-30 minutes. During the 30 minute session the interviewer can assess seven areas to determine a candidate's suitability for a position. Listed are strategies to help you effectively prepare for your interview.

Six Things You Should Know Before Your Telephone Interview

1. Prepared and Professional

- Treat the telephone interview the same as the face-to-face interview.
- Although you may not be dressed in business attire do not let your "relaxed image" come through in your telephone conversation.

2. Interview Documents

Near each telephone you should have the following interview documents.

1. Ink pen and writing tablet

2. Resume

3. Employment dates for each position

4. Salary history for each position

5. Complete business address and telephone number of each employer

6. Why you left each employer

7. Explain any employment gaps

8. Have your calendar or appointment book available to schedule a face-to-face interview

3. Answer the Telephone

- Answer the telephone with an upbeat simple "hello" or "hello this is [your name]"
- Do not answer the telephone if you are not prepared for the call. Let the call go to voice mail

– get organized and call your contact back within an hour – timing is everything.

4. Intelligent Questions

- Have a list of well prepared questions to ask about the position.

5. Company Research

- Be prepared to answer the question "What do you know about XYZ Company?"

6. Negative Questions

- Anticipate negative questions so you can be prepared with positive answers. For example:

Interviewer: "I see you have a history of changing jobs every two years or less can you tell me what happened"?

Interviewee: "Unfortunately I was downsized from the last two companies I worked for. I realize this was a business decision and had nothing to do with my abilities."

Interviewer: "I see on your resume you got out of the Military last year. Can you tell me what you have been doing since your departure from Military service?

Interviewee: I spent time looking for employment and volunteering in my community as…." or "I took college courses at XYZ College or University to improve my skills to gain employment" or I took an internship at XYZ Company to learn new skills and improve existing skills in…."

At the end of the telephone interview be sure to have your interviewers complete contact information.

Seventeen Tips to Prepare For a Successful Interview

1. Privacy

- Be in a private, quite and comfortable place where you feel comfortable having a business conversation.

2. Organize your Thoughts

- Answer questions just as you would during a face-to-face interview. Organize your thoughts and answers and ask for clarification about questions you do not understand.
- Focus on your strengths and qualifications for the job and be prepared to overcome objections about your abilities, by providing examples of your skills.

3. Practice

- Practice "out loud" what you are going to say with a friend or by yourself. By doing this you get to hear how you sound and can make changes.

4. Self Confident Voice

- Have a self confident an enthusiastic voice.

5. Smile

- Smiling when you talk helps your personality come through.

6. Yes or No Answers

- Avoid yes or no answers – add information to your response.

7. How to Speak

- Speak slowly and directly into the telephone.

8. Avoid Dead Telephone Conversation Time

- Don't allow dead air time – have general filler conversation.

9. Listen

- Listen carefully to questions asked.

10. Call Waiting

- Do not interrupt your conversation during the interview let your phone call go to voice mail.
- Placing an interviewer on hold is unprofessional and shows a lack of business etiquette.

11. Cordless and Cell Phones

- Be aware these telephones require charging. Avoid using these phones if at all possible.

12. Contact Information

- Use the *interviewer's name* during your interview conversation makes it more personal.

13. Telephone Body Posture

- Sit in an upright position or stand whichever is the most comfortable for you.

14. Nervous Habits

- Avoid nervous habits such as, clicking a pen or heavy breathing.

15. Drinking Water

- To clear your throat, do not turn on the water tap use bottle water instead. Drink quietly while the other person is speaking.

16. Prepare as You Would for a Face-to-Face Interview

- Be prepared for the telephone interview just as you would for a face-to-face.

17. Next Step

- At the end of your conversation be sure you understand the interview process.
- Close by asking for the job – wait for a response – then ask "What is the next step in the interview process?"

Seven Evaluation Factors of a 30-Minute Telephone Interview

1. Communication

- How well do you communicate your thoughts?

2. Positive Attitude

- Is your conversation upbeat and positive?
- Did you thank the caller for contacting you?
- Did you make small conversation before you began?

3. Quick Thinker

- Are you able to think quickly on your feet to answer questions about your background?

4. Knowledge

- Can you answer their questions?
- What do you know about XYZ Company without stumbling?

5. Criticism

- Can you accept criticism about your background without becoming defensive, rude or unprofessional?

6. Problem Solving

- Can you confidently describe the process you use to solve problems?

- Have you prepared a "short story" to use while you are on the phone?

7. Right Fit

- Are you the right fit for the position and culture?

Based on how well you communicate your answers the interviewer will determine if you will proceed to the next step in the interview process.

Five Telephone Evaluation Points You Need to Pass

1. Voice

- Did you have an enthusiastic and sincere voice?

2. Questions

- Did you answer questions directly or vaguely?
- Did you ask questions about the career opportunity?

3. Company Research

- Did you ask simple questions that would have been available during your company search?

4. Career Opportunity

- Did you pursue the career opportunity by a phone call or a job search website?

5. Professional Documents

- Did the potential employer have your resume and portfolio ahead of time?

Many interviewers use the same criteria to evaluate candidates after a face-to-face interview, therefore knowing how to interview effectively for both types of interviews will be beneficial.

What to Do After Your Telephone Interview

1. Notes

- Take notes about what was discussed and the next step. Date your notes for easy reference.

2. Thank You Letter

- Type a thank you letter to the interviewer stating key points about your skills and interest in the position.

3. Overcome a Unsuccessful Interview

- Call or email the interviewer the next business day and say you forgot to mention a project, special assignment or skill that would be beneficial for the position.
- Include information you omitted in your telephone conversation as one of the key points in your thank you letter.

Interview Body Language

The Body Speaks Louder Than Your Words

INTRODUCTION

What does your body language say about you? Although it's best to know how to answer the typical interview questions, don't forget to pay attention to your non-verbal communication during your interview. Your body language speaks louder than your words.

Studies have shown employers form an impression of you within the first ten minutes of your interview. About 93% of what you communicate is not with words but your professional image and your voice.

The best way to prepare for your interview is to be aware of your interview body language. Practicing in front of a mirror will help you communicate the right body language. The goal is to be confident and professional.

Everyone sends involuntary messages to the interviewer. What should you do? Listed are non-verbal communication tips to give you the career advantage.

Interview Body Language

1. Be Sincere

- Greet your interviewer with a smile and engage them with direct eye contact.
- Maintaining good eye contact shows respect and interest.
- Say something like, "It's a pleasure to meet you" this is a positive first impression.

2. Good Posture

- Good posture is imperative during your interview.
- You should sit up tall with your shoulders back. This allows you to feel confident, in control and relaxed.
- Do not sit on the edge of your chair this could indicate you are nervous and tense.

3. Eye Contact

- Eye contact is essential to establish rapport with your interviewer.
- A lack of eye contact makes the interviewer feel disconnected from you. Make regular eye contact to show you are actively involved in the interview.
- Direct eye contact shows your interviewer you are actively listening.
- Avoid starring or aggressively blinking. Hold eye contact for about 10 seconds briefly looking away then re-establishing eye contact.

- Eye contact is a positive and important aspect of your interview body language when used properly.

4. Insincere Eye Contact

- If you constantly look downwards it makes you appear insincere, unless you are making brief notes or referring to information you have.
- Prior to taking any notes ask for permission from your interviewer.

5. Group Eye Contact

- At group interviews maintain eye contact first with the person asking the question, then glancing periodically at the other interviewers.
- Complete your response by looking at the person who asked the question.

6. Head Posture

- Tilting your head to one side comes across as friendly and open, on the other hand keeping it straight may come across as authoritative and self assured.

7. Control your Arms and Hands

Do you talk with your hands?

If you are unsure what to do with your hands rest them on your lap or under the table. Avoid placing your hands and arms on the interviewer desk or table. Every movement you make with your hands or arms when visible will attract the attention of the interviewer. Control your hands by being aware of what you do with them.

- Do not cross your arms over your chest this signals you are bored, closed, disinterested or defensive.
- Keep your hands away from your face.
- Do not put your hands behind your head.
- Waving your hands and arms can indicate lack of professionalism and uncertainty.
- The less you move your arms or hands indicates you are more confident and in control.
- Practice a comfortable way for you to place your arms and hands when you are sitting at a table.

8. Finger Gestures

- Your fingers when in a steeple position conveys a sign of power and can make you appear arrogant.
- Never point your index fingers like shooters – this indicates aggressive messages to the interviewer.

9. Crossing Leg over Thigh

- Do not cross your leg over your thigh, this is a sign of power and also creates a wall between you and your interviewer.
- Keep your feet flat on the floor or cross them at your ankles might be more comfortable and conveys a confident and professional look. However, crossing and uncrossing them can be distracting if your legs are visible.

10. Vocal Tone

- Speak in a clear and confident tone.

11. Monotone

- Avoid speaking in a monotone voice by varying your tone and pitch.
- Do not come across as emotional and overly excited.

12. Breathe

- Breathe, pause and focus before you answer a question.

13. Interact

- Interact with the interviewer as an equal not a subordinate.

14. Excess Personal Energy

- Excess personal energy can indicate you are nervous or not at ease.
- Be conscious of your need to touch your ears, face, mouth, throat and fidget in your seat. These unconscious signals can hinder your ability to establish trust and credibility.

Problem Solving Interview Strategy
Problem, Action and Results (PAR'S)

INTRODUCTION

A problem-solving interview strategy requires good preparation. First, understand your background and experiences and how they have prepared you to present your problem-solving ability in an effective manner. Second, prepare and practice problem-solving benefit statements. Finally, communicate your transferable skills confidently.

Do you know how to communicate your problem solving skills?

The most effective way to present your problem-solving skills is to review your accomplishments and develop "short stories" or "paint the picture" of your accomplishments. Describe a "problem" you solved, the "action" you took and the "results" of your action. When you tell a "short story" describe the problem, action and results. Clearly speak each of these words so the interviewer will easily be able to follow you and understand your problem-solving process.

A potential employer will usually ask a series of "situational" questions about how you solve problems. Using the PAR Formula you can easily communicate how you define a problem, develop an action plan, and evaluate results.

The PAR Formula

Problem: Define the problem clearly. Set priorities and develop a strategy to address the problem.

Example: The **problem** I had was...

Action: Develop an action plan. Discuss the steps you used to achieve the plan.

Example: The **action** I took was...

Results: How well did you solve your problem? What did you learn that will be beneficial to solve or eliminate future problems?

Example: As a **result** of my action...

Prior to your interview write down and memorize three to six examples of PAR'S and practice them so you can confidently describe a problem-solving "situational" question without hesitation.

Consider the following **PAR** actions steps when preparing for your interview.

Problem You Encountered

- What was the problem?
- Describe a non-routine challenging problem.
- Did you identify the problem yourself or was it brought to your attention?

Action You Took To Solve the Problem

- How did you proceed?
- What specifically did you do?
- Present any creative or innovative skills.
- Describe what steps you took and how you did it.
- Emphasize what was done under your supervision.
- Describe the challenges encountered and how you overcame them.

Results You Achieved

- What did you accomplish?
- Describe your achievements and contributions.
- Specify what department or division benefited.
- How did they benefit and by how much?

Listed is a **PAR** guide to help you complete the process.

"Paint A Picture" of Your Knowledge, Skills and Abilities

Problem   _____

Action   _____

Results   _____

Summary

Do you provide examples of your transferable skills?

Your problem-solving preparation will demonstrate your ability to solve problems. When you identify a skill that is required for a position always provide an example by telling a "short story" of how you use that skill at work. Using this strategy will separate you from other candidates that have similar skills and credentials.

The interviewer wants to see your transferable skills in the position you are applying for. The only way to communicate your skills and increase your chances of landing the job is to provide "examples" of your abilities.

Without providing examples you become just another candidate. The PAR Formula allows you the ability to differentiate your skills in an easy yet effective process and position you as a serious candidate of interest.

The Power of Personal Branding

A Career Distinction Tool

INTRODUCTION

Do you have a personal brand? Personal branding should be used by everyone, new professionals, experienced professionals and those returning to the workplace. A personal brand is a "career distinction" that identifies and differentiates you from other candidates and colleagues in your industry with similar knowledge, skills and abilities.

With personal branding you are the brand. A brand advantage is a unique combination of your education, business qualifications, professional qualifications, internships, volunteer work and work experience you promise to those who hire you.

To attract the ideal employer use strategies to build your personal brand and position you for career success. To "stand out" during your interview communicate to an employer what makes your brand distinct, unique, exceptional, compelling, engaging and valuable to their organization. Provide examples of your strengths, achievements and how you solve problems – the perceived value you will bring to their organization.

Fifteen Strategies to Build Your Personal Brand

Strategy 1: Vision and Purpose

What is your vision and purpose?

- Vision. Identify career strategies that will help you achieve your vision and goals for your future.
- Purpose. Use your career distinction to serve your purpose, stand out, help others and fulfill you life.

Strategy 2: Visual Brand – Appearance

Your visual brand sends a non-verbal message how successful you are.

What does your visual brand – say about you?

- Make a powerful first – visual impression and be consistent with your image.
- Reinforce your personal brand by aligning your appearance with your unique promise of value.
- Wear signature accessories.
- Your body language, gestures and posture all communicate your personal brand.
- Your visual brand should communicate success.
- How distinct is your visual brand from others?
- How do others perceive your visual brand?
- Is your visual brand memorable?

Strategy 3: Branding Tools for Success

Never underestimate the importance of using branding tools for success they communicate your personal brand.

- Use a quality brand ink pen and pencil set. Use black ink for business.

- Does your cell phone style and ring tone communicate your business brand?

- An electronic calendar is recommended. Use a paper calendar as a backup for important dates due to technology failures.

- Does your computer and cell phone screen saver communicate your brand?

- Use a writing portfolio in black or dark brown leather with business card holders.

- Use white tablet paper for business and yellow paper if you are in the legal or financial industry.

- Always carry your personal business cards and business card holder.

- Write your personal branding statement on the back of your business card.

- Do not use a printing card service that prints "free" on the back of your card – this diminishes your brand. Pay extra and write your personal brand statement or leave it blank.

- Present your resume, cover letter and references in a presentation portfolio with your personal business card on the *outside* of the portfolio when you interview.

- Identify a creative way to include your personal brand in emails, reports, and presentations.

Strategy 4: Career Distinction

Think of yourself as a brand. What makes brand YOU unique from brand X?

- What makes your brand unique from your colleagues and competition?
- Does your brand statement include qualities that make you distinctive from others? What are they?
- What is your brand strategy to make you "stand out" from others?
- What are your top three strengths?
- Stand out by leveraging your strengths.
- What is your development plan to gain new skills and improve your brand?
- What is your most worthy personal brand trait?
- What strategy do you use to problem solve?
- What strategies do you implement to complete projects on time and within your assigned budget?
- What positive attributes do others use to describe you?
- Does your email signature communicate your brand?
- Do you write your own quotes or use those written by others?
- Does your voice mail message communicate your brand?

Strategy 5: Career Investment

Career investment is an ongoing process that will enhance your knowledge, skills, expand your network and help you sell your brand to potential employers.

- Read books, articles, and blogs and subscribe to industry newsletters that relate to your industry.

- Attend seminars to increase your industry knowledge.
- Teach a class at a college or university to expand your network and gain recognition for your brand.
- Consider certifications, certificates or an advanced degree to position you for brand distinction.
- Do not settle for where you are today – make a commitment to lifelong learning.

Strategy 6: Communication

- Exceptional active listening, oral and written communication skills will enable you to communicate your brand with confidence and excitement.
- Your resume and cover letter language should compliment each other and support your personal brand.
- Effectively communicating your brand will enable others to support you in achieving goals.
- Be consistent in your brand message.
- Be actively visible to your target employers.
- Be a giver – become a resource for others.
- Write articles to market your brand to gain the attention of key decision makers.
- Create a personal website to establish an online brand presence.
- Identify speaker opportunities to enhance and communicate your brand.
- Volunteer to be on committee or board member to gain exposure for your brand.

Strategy 7: Loyalty

Your reputation for loyalty will follow you throughout your career and has a direct impact on your personal brand. Loyalty is essential to your success. People who can influence others about your loyalty are:

- Colleagues
- Competition
- Co-workers
- Customers
- Industry Contacts

Strategy 8: Perception

- How do others see you as a brand?
- Does your brand live up to its expectations?

Strategy 9: Positioning

- Position yourself to be seen and heard by others.
- Be seen as committed, helpful and knowledgeable about your industry.
- Be known as someone who has an engaging personality, respected, and trusted and a resource for industry advice.
- Be aware of your business etiquette, mannerisms and manners – others will observe your behavior.

Strategy 10: Power of Reputation

- A good reputation is earned by brand management and will follow you throughout your career.

- Your brand reputation should add unique value in your area of expertise.

- Employers want to be associated with a brand that is different and has a strong reputation.

- Develop new skills, expertise and expand your network to grow your brand.

- Seek feedback from co-workers, colleagues, friends, Military contacts and industry experts to determine how others perceive your personal brand. Use feedback to evaluate your brand and position yourself for success.

- Visit social websites regularly to monitor, protect your reputation and ensure you make a good impression to potential employers.

Strategy 11: Self-Value

- Be prepared to turn down career opportunities presented to you that are below your value to maintain and build your brand.

- Know your worth in the marketplace.

- Know your competition so you can focus on those things that are unique about you.

Strategy 12: Signature – Unique Statement

- Write a "brand Statement" in 15 words or less that makes you unique.

Strategy 13: Verbal Brand

- Use word of mouth marketing to share your career success stories with your brand community

– co-workers, colleagues, industry contacts and competitors.

Strategy 14: Visibility Campaign

The most effective way to increase your visibility is to get your name out in the industry. Establish a visibility campaign by:

- Maintaining and expanding your network of colleagues, clients, customers, friends, and industry contacts.
- Attend and speak at industry conferences and meetings.
- Participate in industry panel discussions.
- Write an online book review on a topic that relates to your industry. This becomes part of your online identity when people search your name.
- Volunteer for industry committees.
- Write an online blog – become known as an industry expert on a topic of your expertise to showcase your work.
- Become cautiously active on social networking sites and connect with industry professionals.
- Write an article in your company newsletter on an industry topic which you have expertise.

Strategy 15: Power of Thank-You in Business

Did you say thank you? A thank-you note is a powerful business tool and gesture of professional courtesy. The regular practice of writing a thank-you note will help you be remembered and enhances your personal brand and chances for success.

- Write a thank-you note to interviewers, managers, co-workers and others.

- An email thank-you lacks formality- however it can be used when time is an issue or email is the best method of communicating.

- Once you have stated "thank-you" in your note or email do not say "thanks again" in your closing.

- Showing gratitude and appreciation by using two simple words "thank-you" has the power to transform your career.

Writing a thank-you is the easiest and most powerful strategy you can use to achieve success. A thank-you card can be displayed on a desk as a reminder of your appreciation and admired by others.

At work and in business a personal thank-you note shows your business etiquette, personal brand, appreciation and professionalism. Never underestimate the power of a thank-you note in business – it never goes without being noticed.

Power of Personal Branding
A Career Distinction Tool

Promise of Value. Deliver a unique promise of value to a potential employer.

Expert. Establish yourself as an expert – speak, write a book, article or a blog.

Relationships. Use your personality to build strong internal and external relationships.

Stand Out. Sell your strengths to employers to stand out from the competition.

Opportunity. Evaluate every career opportunity presented to you with an open mind.

Negotiate. In business – you get what you negotiate.

Appearance. Be consistent in your image – Appearances DO Count!

Loyalty. Loyalty is essential to people who support your brand community.

Business Tools. Business tools communicate and enhance your brand.

Reputation. Manage your reputation – it communicates your brand.

Attributes. Listen to positive attributes others use to describe you.

Network. Network with colleagues, co-workers, competitors and industry experts.

Distinction. Career distinction positions you to stand out and build your brand.

Intellectual. Personal and intellectual assets makes you valuable, memorable and in demand.

New. The new economy creates opportunities to leverage your strengths.

Goals. Goals enable you to focus and determine your career destination.

Summary

Personal Branding is building a brand personality. Your brand is your personal and intellectual assets used to differentiate you from others. Whether you are looking for a new job or seeking a promotion build your brand and career distinction. Communicate your unique promise of value to a potential employer. Manage your brand reputation, professional appearance, platform, online presence and brand community.

Today every career advantage counts – use these innovative strategies as a career distinction tool that will position you to stand-out in today's competitive market.

STRATEGY NINETEEN

Ask For The Job™

A Powerful Career Strategy for Employment

INTRODUCTION

The most important step in the interview is the closing process – your goal is to leave the interviewer with the impression you are the only candidate for the job. To gain the job offer – prepare your closing pitch, consider the company, position, interviewer's style, your personal style and your purpose for being there.

Many professionals do not Ask For The Job™ which is a signal to the hiring manager you are not sure whether you want the job. Asserting yourself and using this unique career strategy shows genuine interest and your ability to "sell yourself" and close the interview.

How do you close the interview? Do you ask for the job?

Never leave an interview without "asking for the job" and finding out what is the next step in the interview process. Asking – only what the next step is will provide you with the formality of steps – *not* the job offer.

To get hired - simply ask the hiring manager *"May I please have this career opportunity"*? Or *"I'm excited about what we discussed today and your confirmation that my skills are the best match for the job requirements, may I please have the job"*?

How you ask for the job will determine how the interviewer will respond. It's not what you say – it's how you say it that matters. When you speak with confidence and sincerity in your voice you are one step closer to landing your dream job.

The Power of Listening

Communication is more about listening and less about talking. The ability to listen during your interview is an important business communication skill. Listening for closing cues and buying signals will alert you to confirmations or objections of your skills and ability to strengthen or overcome them.

Listen for Closing Cues

- Listen for confirmation of your knowledge, skills and abilities and ability to solve problems.
- Listen for objections or "red flags" about your abilities and overcome them by providing specific examples of your skills.
- *When you do not overcome objections to your skills, you eliminate yourself from the interview process.* In the interviewer's mind the interview is over.

Listen for Buying Signals

- We want you. "I see you will be a great fit in…"
- They see your skills in the position. "We are looking for a person with your specific skill set."
- They close you – the interviewer tells you the benefits of your skills in their organization. "We need a person on our team that has your expertise and credentials that will give us the leverage we need over our competitors."

Timing Your Close

- Timing is everything – when the buying signals are in your favor – do not wait – close the interview –"Ask For The job™." Once you ask for the job – remain silent until your interviewer responds.

Interview Closing Rules

Your interview closing will position you to stand out as a professional. The best way to close the interview is to follow interview closing rules.

Nine Interview Closing Rules

Rule 1 – Ask Questions

- Ask your prepared uncommon questions about the company, job and management.

Rule 2 – Reinforce Your Strengths

- Reinforce your skills by providing examples. Without examples you are just another candidate.

- Briefly summarize and sell your key strengths that will position you as the only candidate for the job.

Rule 3 – Address Interviewers Questions

- Address and overcome concerns or weaknesses the interviewer has about your ability to perform the job. You can do this by listening, observing the interviewers body language, facial expression and by asking "Do you have any questions that I can address for you?" This allows the interviewer time to express concerns they have about your ability to perform the job.

- Overcome objections by giving *examples* of your strengths in a specific area.

- If your interviewer has identified a weakness which is important for the job, it's essential you state what strategies you are implementing to improve your skills.

- Once you state your strategy to overcome concerns you gain the support of the hiring manager. For example, if your weakness is organizational skills, you might say you use a planner to list important dates or projects, you create a daily "to do list" and plan ahead to ensure projects or reports are completed on time.

Rule 4 – Express Your Enthusiasm

- Express your enthusiasm for the position and company.

Rule 5 – Ask For The Job™ – Interview Closing Strategies

- Ask for the job each time you are interviewed whether it is by an individual or panel.

- Always close – never leave assumptions you want the job.

- Never stop closing until you gain a job offer.

- Close with a "commitment" – ask about the next step in the interview process.

- Close the interview by "asking for the job."

- Interview Goal – The goal of your interview is to end on affirmations. The more "yes" statements of agreement, the closer you get to a secure a job offer. For example: "Mr. Greene would you agree my skills and experience are the best match for this position"? Asking three "yes" questions will position you for the close.

- Psychology – The psychology behind asking "yes" questions is people prefer to be agreeable. Few people enjoy saying "no." The best way to avoid saying "no" is by saying, "yes."

- Yes Responses – If your interviewer responds by saying, "yes" to your questions, ask your last question whether explicitly or implicitly:

"May I please have the job?"

OR

"I think you confirmed in my questions that I'm the most qualified person for this career opportunity. I would like to join your team."

"May I please have the career opportunity"?

Do not say a word. Silence is powerful. Wait for the interviewer to respond to your question.

Rule 6 – The Next Step

- Ask about the next step in the interview process so you will know what to expect for a second interview, assessments, a physical etc.

- Establish a time frame you can expect to hear from the interviewer or when you can follow-up on your interview status.

Rule 7 – Thank the Interviewer

- Thank the interviewer for the time they have spent with you.

- Give a firm handshake, smile and make confident eye contact with the interviewer.

- Ask for the interviewer's business card so you can send a thank you letter.

Rule 8 – Thank –You Letter

- Send an email thank you letter to your interviewers and reinforce your strengths they identified would be of value in short bullet points.

- A thank you letter is recommended over a thank you note – it allows you to continue to "sell" your skills to a potential employer.

- A thank you note does not allow adequate space for you to reinforce skills discussed during the interview that are valuable to the employer.

Rule 9 – Follow-up

- Follow up to determine the results of your interview.

The Power of a Thank-You Letter

INTRODUCTION

Did you write a thank you letter? Sending a thank-you letter after an interview shows your professionalism and respect. This gesture of business etiquette may give you the job edge over other applicants. Statistics have shown applicants who send a thank-you letter following an interview may increase their chances of a second interview and possibly landing the job offer. Many managers support thank-you letters however, it is estimated approximately forty-nine percent of applicants don't take time to send them. A thank-you letter should only be a few short paragraphs in length with easy to read bullets to point out your skills for the position. The thank-you letter allows you the ability to accomplish:

Three Key Interview Objectives:

1. **Express** appreciation for the interview.

2. **Reinforce** your interest and qualifications for the job in bullet format.

3. **Close** by expressing the value your skills will bring to the organization and why they should hire you.

4. Listed are a few tips to consider the next time you compose a thank-you letter following your job interview.

Six Thank-You Letter Tips

1. Specific Points

- Identify specific points your interviewer was impressed with about your background during your interview conversation. For example, if the employer mentioned multiple times your project management expertise and certifications would be valuable to their organization, use the thank-you letter to remind them of what they liked about your qualifications.

2. Multiple Thank-yous'

- It's commonplace for many employers to involve multiple people during the hiring process. If you were interviewed with more than one person each person should receive a slightly different thank-you letter, as managers often compare letters.

- Ask for a business card from each person at the close of your interview. If they don't have business cards be sure to write down their full names or call back and ask the receptionist for the names, correct spelling and titles of each person.

3. 24-Hour Rule

- Its recommended applicants email a formal thank-you letter within 24 hours. If you have traveled from out of state mail the original thank-you letter within 48 hours.

- An email thank-you letter is appropriate especially if a hiring decision will be made within three business days or if you know your contact will be on travel.

- Type your thank-you letter on quality stationery – this gives you the ability to reiterate your skills in a bullet format, a hand-written note is not advisable for this reason.

- Perception is important and can work against you if your handwriting is not favorable. The risk is not worth it.

4. Be Hopeful

- Although you might have doubts about the success of your interview it's advisable to send a thank-you letter.

- Your display of professionalism could work in your favor or at a future date.

5. The Competitive Edge

- Anything you can do to gain the attention of the hiring committee will be to your advantage. Sending a compelling thank-you letter could be the one thing that gives you the competitive edge over other applicants.

6. Take Notes

- Taking notes after an interview will help you remember key factors about your interview, and who said what - that can be incorporated in your thank-you letter.

Five Simple Thank You Letter Strategies

1. Professional Etiquette and Respect

- Sending a thank-you letter shows the interviewer(s) your professional etiquette and respect.

2. Stand Out

- The fact that many job applicants don't send thank-you letters you automatically stand out from the crowd.

3. Reiterate Key Points

- A thank-you letter gives you another opportunity to mention key points you made and the interviewer liked about your skill set.

4. Key Points You Forgot

- A thank-you letter allows you to include key points you forgot to mention during your interview that are essential to the position.

5. Written Communication Skills

- A thank-you letter allows you to demonstrate your written communication skills that are vital for business.

Summary

Writing a thank-you letter makes a big difference to a potential employer. Thank-you letters are not difficult or time consuming. When you don't send one and your competition does this sends a non-verbal message about your professionalism. Sending a thank-you letter could be the difference between the job going to you or someone else. Send a thank-you letter and make sure the job offer goes to you.

The Power of Salary Negotiation

INTRODUCTION

Are you confident negotiating your salary package? Salary negotiation is an essential skill that all professionals should possess. Many professionals are uncomfortable negotiating their salary and benefits package – as a result they often accept a salary lower than what they are worth. Unlike the Military – in the civilian job market in most career opportunities you can negotiate your salary package.

Although there has been a trend of fixed salaries do not let that stop you from asking a potential employer if there is room for negotiation. You will not know what your negotiating power is until you ask for a higher salary – the goal is not to leave money on the table. An employer will respect you for asking and not assuming you have no negotiating power. Effective salary negotiation skills will ensure you will receive top salary and benefits for your knowledge and work experience.

Visual Presentation and Perception Add Value

At your final interview you will probably meet with one or more multiple managers or a company executive. Create a perception of value in your appearance and use business tools that make you stand out and more valuable than your competition.

Dress for Success – Professional Appearance

- Dress in a quality business suit for your final interview and possible job offer – show your value – perception is everything.

Resume Portfolio

- Put your resume, references and other essential documents in a portfolio with your personal business card on the *outside* of the portfolio.

Writing Tablet and Pen

- Pull out your leather writing tablet and quality ink pen even though you do not need to write anything down – perception of your business tools add value to your offer.

Final Interview Thank-You

After your final interview send an *email* thank you letter immediately to your contacts. Call – *do not* email the contacts that previously interviewed you – timing is everything. Thank your interviewers for their support during the interview process and inform them when the final decision will be made.

This strategy will effectively position you as a top candidate, raise the bar and expectations for other candidates. When the interviewers make their hiring decision you will have made a lasting impression. They will remember you – your skills and the professionalism you demonstrated during the interview process. Listed are salary negotiation strategies to use prior to your job offer.

Salary Negotiation Strategies

1. Research – Know What You Are Worth

- Do your research to determine what the current salary range is for someone with your knowledge, skills, abilities and education in your current market.

2. Salary Range

Never state the salary you want without knowing the range.

- The unspoken rule is the first person who states an amount loses their negotiation power. *Always* ask what the salary range is before you state a desired amount. Listed is an example to illustrate what can happen when you request a salary without the knowledge of a salary range.

Candidate 1:

Hiring Manager: What salary are you expecting for this position?

Candidate: I would like a base salary of $50,000 per year – plus benefits.

Hiring Manager: Great, I accept your salary request and will prepare the letter of offer for you.

Candidate 2:

Hiring Manager: What are your salary expectations for this position?

Candidate: Could you share with me what the salary range is for this position?

Hiring Manager: Yes, the salary range is between $50,000 - $60,000 per year – plus benefits.

Candidate: Based on the value of my experience you discussed during my interviews – I believe $60,000 is appropriate.

Although your salary might not start at $60,000 per year – starting at the top of the range increases your chances of negotiating a desired income based on your ability to perform the job and sell your skills. When you state a lower salary figure without knowledge of the range it's difficult to increase what you initially stated you wanted. You have also communicated your lack of negotiation skills by stating a figure before you know the details of the offer.

Candidate 1 possibly has lost $10,000 per year – if you were employed for a minimum of two years a salary loss of $20,000.00. Your goal is to get paid for what you are worth – the hiring manager's goal is to hire the most qualified candidate at the least amount of cost to their organization.

3. Always Negotiate the Salary Offer

- If you are offered a salary, always ask for more than you are offered – you will be respected for it.

4. Take Risks in Negotiation

- Be prepared to confidently provide examples of why you add value to the position and want more money.

5. Know When To Stop Negotiations

- Do not engage in a salary war at the risk of losing the support of the employer or the job offer.

6. New Hire Bonus

- Once your salary is negotiated ask if there is a "new hire" bonus – a secret in the industry that no one will tell you. Not all companies have a new hire bonus – however you will not know unless you ask.

7. Severance Policy

- Changes in the new economy can bring about unforeseen changes for organizations as result the employer may need to reorganize and downsize.
- Ask your employer if they have a severance policy for employees who are downsized. If they do – ask for a copy for your files, if not ask to have a severance agreement included in your letter of offer.
- A severance agreement discussed during the new hire process provides "piece of mind" at an "emotional" time when you are faced with unemployment.

8. Job Offer – Get it in Writing

- Always get the job offer – position title, salary, bonus and commission program, benefits and start date in writing before you give notice at your current employer if you are employed.

Summary

Every professional should be capable of negotiating their salary and benefits. Each interview leading up to your job offer should be strategically planned. Your salary expectations should be negotiable based on your skill set and the current job market. The goal of salary negotiations is for both parties to give and take for a successful outcome.

STRATEGY TWENTY TWO

Job Search

Stay on Track

Eleven Tips to Stay on Track

Tip 1: Search for employment opportunities everyday.

Tip 2: Transferable skills are your most valuable assets to get hired.

Tip 3: Ask For The Job™ when presented with a career opportunity you want.

Tip 4: You are accountable and responsible for your career success.

Tip 5: Opportunities are in traditional and non-traditional career paths.

Tip 6: Network with family, friends, past employers, Military and community contacts.

Tip 7: Treat every job lead as a possible opportunity for employment.

Tip 8: Research companies before you have a telephone or face to face interview.

Tip 9: Arrive 20 minutes early for scheduled interview appointments.

Tip 10: Courage is essential to achieve goals.

Tip 11: Knowledge is your ability to control your future.

Military to Civilian Transition

Job Search Strategies and Tips to Get Hired in the Civilian Job Market

Summary

Are you interviewing? Have you received a job offer or promotion?

If you answered no to one of these questions – it's time to re-evaluate your current job search plan and implement job search strategies in *Military to Civilian Transition*. A competitive market requires exceptional interview skills to land a new career.

A large pool of candidates are actively interviewing and seeking the job you want. Make a commitment to plan, prepare and execute an effective interview strategy that will have a life-changing effect on your career, income and future.

It's essential to make a powerful first impression so you will be invited for a second interview. Your resume, cover letter, telephone and face-to-face interviews are used to evaluate your employment, listening, written and oral communication skills.

Military to Civilian Transition provides strategies, tips, tools, and rules to enable you to be successful at interviewing. Use new business tools, ask intelligent interview questions, and tell short stories how your transferable skills can be of value to XYZ Company. Use the PAR formula to effectively communicate how you solve problems and incorporate personal branding strategies to make you stand out.

The goal of interviewing is to gain the job offer. The most important strategy you can use at the end of your interview is to – Ask For The Job™. The stakes are high – this unique interview strategy will position you to close the deal.

Military to Civilian Transition: Job Search Strategies and Tips to Get Hired in the Civilian Job Market is the ultimate career resource written for you to provide leading-edge strategies you can use to compete and get hired in the civilian job market.

Write A Book Review:

You are invited to write a book review at:

www.amazon.com and www.barnesandnoble.com

Thank you for sharing your feedback.

Email Me:

Do You Have Interview Questions or Success Stories to Share?

You are invited to email me at:

Patricia@militarytociviliantransition.net

Thank you for your time.

Military to Civilian Transition
Job Search Booklets

Job Search Booklets

1. Power Interview Image

2. Power Interview Etiquette: 17 Rules for Interviewing

3. 17 Powerful Interview Questions

4. Power Business Meals: Dining Etiquette

5. Power Business Image: Show You Mean Business

6. Power of Employment: 27 Secrets to Survive Your First 90 Days of Employment

7. Networking: 17 Essential Strategies for the 21st Century

8. Power Business Casual: Show You Mean Business

9. Power Career Fairs: Making Connections Face-to-Face

10. Power of Personal Branding: A Career Distinction Tool

11. Power of Professionalism

Titles: One or multiple titles can be ordered

Purchases: Minimum order – 50 Booklets Per Title

Booklets: Print-On-Demand

Discounts for Bulk Purchases: Minimum Order 350 Booklets

Information: Discounts for bulk purchases please contact Patricia Dorch

Email: Patricia@militarytociviliantransition.net

Website: www.militarytociviliantransition.net

ABOUT THE AUTHOR

PATRICIA DORCH is President and CEO of EXECU DRESS. She has a Master of Science in Business Organizational Management from the University of LaVerne - LaVerne, California and undergraduate degrees from Pratt Institute and Fashion Institute of Technology in New York.

Patricia has a Business and Business Image background with over 20 years of work experience in the Corporate America in Sales and Marketing. Her civilian two year tour of duty working with Military personnel and dependents on a Military base in Sicily, Italy uniquely positions and qualifies her to train Military to Civilian Transition – Job Search Skills, Personal Branding Strategies, Professionalism, Business and Business Casual attire appropriate for today's workplace.

Patricia is an Author, National Speaker and a Career Expert. Patricia provides Job Search Seminars and Career Advice for *Military to Civilian Transition, College Graduates, 40 Plus and Teen job seekers.*

Patricia is the Author of *Professionalism: New Rules for Workplace Career Success, Job Search: New Get Hired Ideas, Tips and Strategies for 40 Plus, Six Figure Career Coaching Advice: The Ultimate Guide To Achieving Success, Job Search: College Graduates New Career Advice, Ideas and Strategies to Get Hired and Job Search: Teen Interview Tips and Strategies to Get Hired.*

Available at: www.amazon.com and

www.barnesandnoble.com

Patricia is an in-demand Career Expert who specializes in maximizing the potential for professionals to get hired, demonstrate professionalism in the workplace and get promoted in today's ultra competitive job market. Patricia has an extraordinary ability to see career opportunities hidden in plain view. Patricia's message is clear – "Take responsibility for your career and brand your professional brilliance for unparallel success." Patricia Dorch has fast become regarded as the voice for Military to Civilian Transition, College Graduates, 40 Plus and Teens for job search, career advice and success.

Services: Speaker / Author Services / Career Expert / Book Signing

Patricia Dorch is a dynamic Speaker and Trainer – schedule her for your next – Job Search, Personal Branding Strategies, Business and Business Casual and Professionalism Seminars for: Military to Civilian Transition, Veterans Events, Career Fairs and other related Training and Conferences.

Website: www.militarytociviliantransition.net

Email: Patricia@militarytociviliantransition.net

Website: www.whatisprofessionalism.com

Email: Patricia@whatisprofessionalism.com

Website: www.workplaceprofessionalism.com

Email: Patricia@workplaceprofessionalism.com

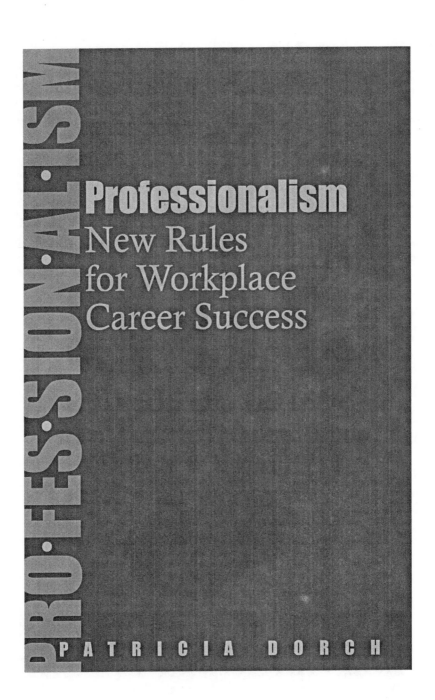

Professionalism
New Rules
for Workplace
Career Success

PATRICIA DORCH

MILITARY TO CIVILIAN TRANSITION
JOB
Search Strategies
and Tips to GET HIRED in the
CIVILIAN JOB MARKET

PATRICIA DORCH

CPSIA information can be obtained at www.ICGtesting.com
Printed in the USA
LVOW10s1318171113

361643LV00015B/773/P

9 780981 685472